# A New
# Outlook

# A New Outlook

NICHOLAS P. SNOEK

Order this book online at www.trafford.com
or email orders@trafford.com

Most Trafford titles are also available at major online book retailers.

Printed in the United States of America.

ISBN: 978-1-4907-1285-7 (sc)
ISBN: 978-1-4907-1284-0 (e)


*Trafford rev. 08/23/2013*

www.trafford.com

**North America & international**
toll-free: 1 888 232 4444 (USA & Canada)
fax: 812 355 4082

**In Dedication To**

**Barbara Pratt-Snoek**

Whose constant prompt proofreading
Was a perpetual blessing

# Introduction

The world as we know it began, to the best of my understanding at the time, somewhere around 1947 CE, two years after dad came home to stay, and regular hours and days made possible a resumption of business in the meat shop at the front of the house, mom and dad again looking after things in general, especially the customers, with Giel helping them in the store, and Mien keeping an eye on kids and things in the rest of the house.

The house cum meatshop was level with the road running along the top of the dike, and the back property sloped down past the orchard and shed right to the edge of the drainage ditch, or sloot, as the Dutch call it.

The front part of the shed was white stucco clean, with high counters along one side, and a machine that spun a large bowl affair while flashing rotary knives minced and then made pudding out of the meat odds and ends that would become sausage. That and a big piston press which would push that mix through a short horizontal pipe into sausage casings, were both on the other side of the working area. And pipe racking all over, along which shiny steel hooks hung, as clean as clean could be.

The back part of the building was full of junk, and provided unlimited accommodation for countless rats, which never seemed to come to the front section, as far as I could tell. One day I saw dad hunkered at the edge of the sloot, and when I came to see, he was watching a rat he had shot, crawling along the muddy far side. "Why don't you shoot it again and kill it?"

"Oh, no need, he's as good as gone already." Yuk. A hard man, my dad. Three times had he been prisoner of war, something to do with the Dutch resistance and the underground—on special assignment, pursuing another sort of rat, as he was heard to say. How on earth did he survive all that?

And more than three times the Hun stompers had gone through the house, searching, while mom sat in a stiff-backed armchair with the six children, five sisters and Erin, close pressed to her intoning the mantra rosary. He knew where dad was, but they never found the hideyhole there, in a cramped spot, squeezing to the outer line of the attic edging over the closet. Hard, not looking there—to not look at the core and tension tip of the crisis minutes. Nor did they find the slaughter space below the shop floor where dad had butchered animals to no end on countless tired nights, making contraband profit all through the war, a desperate black market in a black underground, creating dark investment for a dim and doubtful future.

Later they would be made to leave that money behind, in a trust fund, in grandpa's keeping. The powers that be had made a number of attempts to confiscate it, as was done in the years after the war to people who could not authenticate funds they had access to. But somehow mom had foiled them every time. By way of technicalities, would you believe— wrong date; wrong time; we were not there that day and here's the proof . . . stuff like that. Sometimes, in underhanded ways, underdogs can fight with city hall.

It was no underdog that was all set to bite him, on delivery one day. But then a voice said, right beside him, "Don't look him in the eye; he will think you want to fight him!" Erin, "What should I do, he bloody well wants to fight me!" The voice "Do nothing. Just look at the ground, off to one side a bit, and don't move." He looked the proper look at the dog, which worked, then turned to see, but no one was there. A vanishing voice, by his ear.

That was the first time she had been so forthcoming, though he didn't get to see her till some days later. That was really weird—he had climbed into the big horse chestnut tree in the back yard, and hid among the leaves, scoping the whole place as he often did, but this time he noticed this girl only a couple of feet away, doing the same thing. "What, who are you?"

"I'm Leukje, that's who I am, and you are Erin." He couldn't believe it. "How do you know that, and why didn't I see you climb up here?" With a shy little smile "I've been around the place for quite a while, so I know the names of the whole family. And you didn't see me climb because I wasn't here till I wanted to be here." Erin "I don't understand! How can you not be here and then just be here, zoom like that?" She, "Don't feel bad, cuz I don't understand it either. Leuk, huh?" "So you are called little joke because you play jokes on people?" "I don't do that. I just am a little joke, Leukje."

"And you can be invisible the same way, by just deciding to be?" "No, silly, there's no deciding, it just happens. If it's better that no one else can see me, then that's what happens." Erin "Then what about hearing you? Seems to me I've heard you once in a while before that dog growled at me." "Yeah, now you're getting the idea. You and I have talked to each other lots, but you just don't remember too much about it." "And you do remember, more than I do?" Leukje "Yes. Lots more, complete memory."

"That doesn't seem fair." "Sure it does, I don't have much else to do, just keep an eye on you." Erin is suddenly called in to supper, so he quickly climbs down. When he looks back up, he sees nothing. "Leukje?" Nothing.

# Chapter 1

## Going to Canada

It's the fall of 1951, seven o'clock of a Saturday morning, and the whole family is standing at the curb waiting for a bus to take them to Paris, France. They will overnight there, then take a train to Le Havre, to embark on an ocean liner, the Ascania. In October—a chilly passage, dank and damp, chugging into winter, vers quelques arpentes de neige. Going to Canada—holy mackerel, what for?

A couple of friends from places nearby wait with them, but little is said—it's all sort of sad and ceremonial. It has come to be real so quickly, this idea of going to Canada. Dad's brother in B.C. is sponsoring them, and has already reserved a job in the meat business. Erin now has six sisters and a brother, Pietje, named after the other grandpa. Leukje has not surfaced for some time, so that's in limbo now as well. Some kind of tragic irony, that an invisible friend should actually be, and persist, invisible. Some rite of passage this is, all at loose ends and out of joint.

The bus comes, the bus goes, and Erin sits with mom. Dad is more towards the back, toning down the others. A family of females—first mom and dad; two girls, a boy Erin; two girls, a boy Piet; two girls, and who knows after that, if there be any after that. This is probably the end of it, as mom gets older bolder.

"Well, Erin, it looks like your 11th birthday will be in Canada, a week before our first Christmas there." "Yup, it does. Providing everything goes as planned."

"Well, why shouldn't it? What could possibly go wrong? Are you worried?"

"Can't help wondering if this is such a good idea, just casting off to go chasing some dream thousands of miles away. What do we know about things over there? We could land in a big pile of trouble." Mom "Oh, come, we're not some ignorant kids on a wild goose chase." He, grinning a bit: "Some of us are."

The whole family is seasick, except mom, and she goes dancing, watches movies, and takes meals on schedule. She tries to look after the others, but appetites are skimpy, and there is little interest in any posture not horizontal. Dad gathers the kids around him on the deck, when possible, and plays phonographic English lessons. Erin is more interested in an attractive young lady displaying herself in a deckchair close by, and, it seems, she in him. They try to talk, but his knowledge of English is limited. Dad observes this, and tries to compensate for Erin's shortcomings, but does little better, especially when mom occasionally comes by. The worst laid plans of boys and men gang aft agley, they say.

Erin's lying down in his cabin, thinking about all this, when suddenly he sees Leukje sitting in the recliner beside the bed. Hot dog! "Hello Erin, how are you?"

"I'm OK, Leukje—been wondering where you got to. Where have you been?"

"Oh, I haven't been anywhere at all, and I did check on you from time to time to see what was going on. You must realize I cannot do too much by myself."

Erin muses about this for a bit, then: "I don't understand. Why not? How does this work?" She: "Come on, what makes you think I know any better? Near as I can figure it out, I am not Leukje until you think some thought or other that pulls me closer." Erin "But I've thought of you often, and haven't seen you at all."

She "You must know from before when we talked about it, that I can be there without your seeing me, and that we can talk when that happens." He: "So why haven't we done that, like we did in Holland?" Leukje looks at him, exasperated. "Did you leave part of your mind over there? Since you started on this silly trip you haven't been alone at all. What would others think if you suddenly started a conversation with empty space?" Erin "Ohh, I see what you mean. You're talking a bit like a guardian angel, you know that?" She: "Why Erin! That's the nicest thing you've ever said to me!" He: "I guess you're not an angel then, are you, guardian or otherwise." She: "Ahah, your mind is catching up and all. But now that we're in sync I shouldn't be mean to you?" He looks puzzled again, frowns.

Erin: "Not really. But while we're on the subject, could we settle what sort of creature you actually are?" She: "Now there you go again. If you just think back a bit you should remember that all such questions have been of little use. I do not know, any more than you do 'what sort of creature' I actually am, and that puts us in the middle of a silly circle, doesn't it?" He: "More like on the edge of one, a bit like being seasick. And what about that, do you get seasick?" Leukje "No, I do not get seasick, since it takes a body, with the attendant and built-in apparatus for deducing states of motion or rest in relation to spatial arrangements vis-a-vis the outside world, to do so."

Erin "Now you're saying you have no body, and here am I, looking at your body, sitting there in my chair." She: "And you really think that I would not know whether I have a body? Perhaps you should add, that you think I have no mind? Here's something else. Do you think that what you see in that mirror over there is a body? If you took a gun and shoot what you see in there, do you suppose the mirror would bleed?" Erin "Obviously, no—the mirror would shatter to pieces." There is a knock at the door.

"Erin, we're going to be in the Halifax port early tomorrow, so mom and dad want us all to get together so we can plan how to be ready for that." Without looking back, he ducks out the door. Bloody hell, it was just getting interesting.

She's like a reflection in a mirror, with no substance at all, a phantasm? Like an afterimage, but one that endures. Weird or what? How can she sit up in a tree, with her dress draped over her knees, and the edges of the dress shifting in the breeze? Is she building all that detail and feeding it to me? Or am I manufacturing the whole thing from scratch without being aware of doing it? What is she?

Maybe we do it together. Hey, that seems to be how it works, the way she says she just sort of finds herself, wherever—and I find her there, wherever. Curious. And I bet if I offer her that as a working hypothesis, she'll just say okay, whatever. She does have a mind of her own, though, even a touch of temper. I suppose the best way to deal with her is gently, not to shunt or shock pure evanescence. More things obtain, dear Erin lad, in heaven and on earth, than your psychologies have dreamt of, let alone mythologies, or personal suppositions and presumptions.

The water is quiet here, like glass. And look! The conifers rise up onto the steep incline of the rock like pointed pikes, and bits of pure white snow are all sugared over the limbs with white candy canes like in a fairytale. How beautiful! If this is a foretaste of Canada, then bring it on, I love it already! Oh, yes, I'm being childlike, but what the heck, am I not a mere child, of 10.11 tender years?

Customs, excise, immigration, formalities legalities and officiousness galore; but there are interpreters, and even moments of sympathetic consideration in this case of such a large family with overtired and stressed out parents, who seem to not even have a steady grasp of their own guttural language. But then, they've never done this sort of thing before. How many families of ten would do this?

Time ticks along and things get done and dusted . . . and somehow, in spite of all the poking, the prodding, and all the halting questions, no one notices the luger, the semiautomatic rifle, or the machine gun, not even the bucket helmet, all of which dad has with some inspired magic touch, secreted among mom's more flouncy and personal garmentry. Although pictures of stressed harassment, they are wishing wells of resourcefulness, these parents of mine! The nerve! The audacity! The toothclenched sore jaw calmness punctuated with anxious looks of piteous helplessness—such drama! Wow. Talk of hidden talents.

It worked, it worked! They're safely on the train, assigned to seats and berths and carry-on cubbyholes, and private portabilities between their feet, just waiting for the whistles and the clunk and clunk clunk of shunting wheels and banging clevices. How strange, in order to get to mainland Canada, we're going to slice through a jutting up pseudopod of the U.S.A., nonstop. How friendly with each other these two pasted together countries must be.

This is a passenger train, so stops are frequent. Each time this happens, mom and dad take turns dashing out to the platform, locating a convenience store, and quickly buying some bread, butter, and various sandwich spreads. And that is the regimen for a whole week, trundling across all of Canada to B.C.

On the second day Erin sits down with mom. "Are we poor now, mom? Have we spent everything just to make the trip?" Mom "Well, not exactly. Cash is a bit awkward, that's all. You know we had to leave the contraband money behind, so available funds got chopped down quite a lot. We had an option to either bring almost all liquid assets in paper or else pack up most of our movable belongings in a big crate and have that shipped over as soon as we get into a house of our own—we'll be staying with Martien and Alie for a while in the meantime." Erin nods: "I see. We just have to put up with all this stuff for the greater good in the long run. It will be nice to have a lot of our own things over there, won't it?"

"Yes. You will be happy that almost all your books are coming over, and the toys for the younger kids." Erin is a voracious reader, so he already had a little library of his own gathered up. Good stuff! And how nice it is that mom talks to him on an adult level. She's been doing that more and more. Quite a compliment.

At one stop dad gets the kids some balloons they can blow up to play with, and soon the whole carload of people is involved in batting the colored blobs around, just to keep them from landing—even businessmen in suits and ties get right into it. And little old ladies, and prim and proper socialites. Keen!

Erin misses Leukje, but he can't do much about it. He consoles himself when he finds there is a shelf of books available to the passengers, and soon he is avidly devouring whatever seems interesting at all. He hadn't come across westerns before, so he gobbles a few of those, as the language is quite simple and down to earth. But when he gets to the stage where he can almost manage by running his eye down the middle of the page he realizes he's not getting much out of them, and turns to more challenging fare. There's another young fellow doing the same, and everyone is quite amused when the conductor, as he walks by, whispers loudly "Has he got it into her yet?" A black man he is, and his voice a good solid baritone, a likable sort. Makes one think of Louis Armstrong.

There's a car switch to do in Winnipeg, and it means they spend a whole day there, waiting. A bit scary, sure hope it all works out. They wander the streets and check out some shops, but mostly they dawdle-wish this hadn't happened. What can you do in a big city besides spend money and time? But, this too passes, and they get on board with some relief, and on they go again.

Yes, on and on and on and over the endless prairies, with the occasional relief provided by a pronghorn antelope, and once, just once, a doe with her young fawn, not far into the field, just looking at the train, totally unconcerned, the fawn not even doing that. Inexhaustible mother nature, providing yet, amen.

Erin had been altar boy for some years, and now he gets to wondering how his Leukje would fit into the catholic scheme of things, and again the question comes niggling at him: what manner of creature was she, is she, or if she IS at all—what ontology is implicate in that sometime visible, oftener invisible little joke?

She is not able to explain her existence to her own satisfaction, much less to mine. What what, what who, what entity could she be? She surely was not born of woman, and given her consciousness, she cannot be some sport of bioscience.

Coming past Calgary they can soon see the foothills of the Rockies in the west, a bit hazy but that improves as they get closer. How on earth will they get up high enough to get to the other side of all that? But, the miles click on and on, and slowly up and up, and eventually they go through Rogers Pass into B.C. and start a gradual descent to the lesser peaks and valleys below. What scenery!

Martien's place is in the southern interior, so several north-south mountain range crossovers later, they eventually get close enough to estimate their eta with some assurance, the target area being more or less halfway between Calgary and the west coast, a sizable city called Chemlupe, on the

Caribou river. About an hour before that, they pass through the town ShallowsArc, at the tip of one arm of Chapcap Lake, and dad tells everyone that there is a slaughterhouse here, and a major meat outlet, owned by two brothers of the man he will be working for at Chemlupe. A bit of a coincidence, in this huge country. Ask the stars why, how.

Having had the foresight to check with the local rail terminal, Martien knew when to expect Piet and family, so with a neighbor and two pickups trucks, he is at the ready by the station, all set to take the in-laws and all their effects to his home, which is right on top of a sandy rise alongside the bank of the Caribou river. And the neighbor's place is not far from his, to boot.

All three families are pretty much in the same age range, so the older girls are able to make friends quite soon, and there is a boy close to Erin's age who does hang out with his newfound cousin for a time, going skating, and watching hockey games, but Erin is less interested in sports and more in competitive board games, chess and checkers, and in reading, in reading almost anything with a bit of grit. For several years he has been borrowing books each Sunday from the church library, and was usually drawn to the more challenging ones. Can't really share that with anyone. Reading is serious. He had noticed that people either read or do not read, and the twain do not much meet.

Leukje soon reappears, and the two soul-associates happily foster and rebuild their relationship. She more and more becomes a person in her own right, less tied to Erin's inner adventures. She even explores for him the countryside and some of the surrounding towns and what happens in the province as a whole.

Christmas is a low key affair, Martien and Alie not being as taken with such things as Piet and Marie, who have always made quite a production out of it.

About a month later it is suddenly decided, between dad's boss and his two brothers, that considering dad's experience in the abattoir division of the meat business, he would be more effective taking over the butchering for the company in ShallowsArc. The offer is made, remuneration agreed on, and another move is in the works. A house is located and rented, a bit small, but the price is good, and off they go. The topography of BC is all mountains and valleys, except in the north where the flatlands of Alberta spread west, and as a result the whole of the westernmost province is a quiltwork of different climates. Chemlupe, for instance, is much drier and colder than ShallowsArc, which is more temperate.

In a couple of weeks the older children are all at school, and settling in nicely in the new digs. When the huge crate comes from Holland everything is ready for that too. Mom no longer has part of a meat business to run, so now she can devote herself to being a mother hen. It must be quite a change for her. She soon starts a small garden as well, as she has a green thumb, and really enjoys it when fresh potatoes, cabbages, and beans gradually become part of the regular fare. She keeps an eye out for opportunities to start some strawberries, and some raspberry and loganberry bushes. Good providers, this old couple—not so old.

The slaughterhouse is down at the edge of the lake, a bit isolated, and most of the time dad works there by himself. Every now and again he brings home a pheasant that he was able to shoot in the corrals where birds come to pick at the grain and other feed that is always on hand for the cows and pigs.

Erin's home room teacher has a talent for languages, and soon has a sort of game going on, with Erin teaching the others Dutch, and they drilling him in the corresponding English expressions. He had hoped there would be French on tap as well, since he had already studied some English and French in Holland, but in the western part of Canada there is less emphasis on French, which is of course more in vogue in the maritime and eastern provinces, especially in Quebec.

Since most of his day is spent in school, and at home the other kids are never far away, he and Leukje have found it necessary to work out a new way for them to communicate— they have conversations without saying the words out loud, having found that if they each just make a point of thinking the words clearly though silently, they can talk much as if they say them. Leukje has found that if she makes herself visible, (only to him,) he can watch her when she mimes as she speaks, a sort of lip reading. This slows down her 'speaking,' but more and more he can speed up his side of it, as she can catch whatever he thinks, quite fast. The biggest temptation is to lapse into voice mode when misunderstandings occur, but soon they get a better handle on that too. Necessity's inventing helps.

It's only another step in the same dynamic that enables her to just 'eavesdrop' when Erin is reading a book, and they can stop to discuss the material anytime, during the reading or afterwards. What fun that can be! More and more they find they see eye to eye an on ever widening range of topics. A bit strange, that.

Time flies, and Erin finds himself in high school. He doesn't care much for sports, partly from being too preoccupied with his own studies, which range outside the school curriculum, and partly because, his right knee being about an inch farther off the ground than his left one, he does not do well in anything that involves running. His reading is stochastically divergent, but in spite of all the distractions, he has no problem maintaining his spot on the academic honor roll.

He's befriended a younger student, Ron, who, having skipped several years, can join Erin in the same classes. Soon they have such a reputation as the school's two geniuses that the counselor gives them permission to attend class or not just as they choose, and they also get the use of a small room just to talk. Ron does not mention being gay, and Erin keeps mum about Leukje.

# Chapter 2

## A Summer Break

About 150 miles south of ShallowsArc sits the mountainside town of Nemson, where an ambitious Christian college has been recruiting students with the aim of qualifying for an association with a university so as to become a degree granting facility. Mom was approached by a couple of young fellows who were doing good works by signing up promising high school graduates to help bring this about.

After a few conversations between mom and Erin it is decided that instead of going for his grade 13 in ShallowsArc, or first year at a university, he might do well to spend a year at the Dutch Reformed college in Nemson, to broaden his horizons, get a taste of education in a more religious environment, all while doing his little bit of good for a worthy cause. Ron, undaunted, will go off to university.

And so it came to pass that Erin took a course in theology, which he quite thoroughly enjoyed, got a good grounding in the sciences and maths, excelled in English literature in that he won a book prize for the most original thinking in that course, had many good talks with the more incisive minds accessible at such a unique campus, and had free rein in a most remarkable library. Leukje helped, but all of this was done without the stimulation and the benefit of Ron's ever combative wide ranging objections to whatever Erin might posit to be a valid and valuable point of contention. A mixed blessing it was, and a sad shortcoming.

But then, every day after classes and before the evening meal he ran his half mile up the mountain, and duly carved a small notch in the limb of a white pine.

Other students at Nemson from this area had carpooled with Erin for the odd weekend home visit, and since he was the more mature and less tempted by the college penchant for a drink or two, he would almost every time be named the designated driver. And so again, partly due to his size, being well over six feet by this time, characteristically Dutch, he is the default leader of the pack.

The years have been rolling along inexorably. The little house in town had proved more irksome than expected, so when dad's increased income from the slaughterhouse position gradually led to some savings, the family started looking for something more spacious. A nearly perfect thirty acre river bottom property just over a mile out of town along the highway came up for sale, with an ample two storey house and a spacious shed. It was ideal. Dad put up the deposit, his boss cosigned for the mortgage, and it was done; everybody was quite happy.

There was a sawmill one hundred yards farther over, so Erin and dad together secured a job pulling lumber, steady nights, with Erin taking the first four hours, and dad the last four. Both of them needed some extra zz's from time to time, but overall it worked out just fine. About a year of that, then something else came up.

The thirty acres being one third poplar bush bordering on the river, one third pasture on the edge of the bush, and one third arable land right along the road, there was an obvious need to provide some shelter for the increasing number of animals that were soon grazing on that fenced in pasture. We needed a barn.

Rumor had it that an old farmer, just a ways back toward town, was going to pull down a big barn he no longer needed, to build a house on the site. Dad had a talk with him, and bought the barn as she stood, for peanuts. Dad was still working at the slaughterhouse, but the unusual pair now quit the sawmill job.

Erin was just starting summer holidays, so several handy Dutch friends and acquaintances were conscripted, and wagonloads of used barn lumber made their way to the needed location. Erin, grade nine, was in charge of the project! Things went along well enough, but it turned out that the roof rafters from the previous barn were only enough to cover the first half of this much bigger one.

Several expeditions were mounted to find young tall cedar trees straight enough to serve for rafters. The trees were found and marked, in the bush above Foothill Rd, the wagon was parked auspiciously camouflaged, and one twilight evening the trees were illegally hand cut, trimmed, and when the dark was deep enough, were brought to their new spots without a hitch. Exactly what a careless speaker might call a godsend. But, it did prove tricky to situate them as needed.

And then, one year later, mom and dad having enquired after the funds that were still in Holland, decided to build their own little meatplant, an abattoir to the back and retail space in the front, all on the far corner of the cultivated field, 600 yards back from the highway. The money came, the building built, and in the fall the business was in bloom—Westside

Meat & Poultry. The two parents were once again partners, providing meat products to the public, and this was the first time Erin was old enough to be of some help in the business. Not that he liked it at all, for even at this age he had become much more a thinker than a doer; by far preferring to dedicate his energy to matters of the mind. Leukje too had been a bit less than content, she having had far fewer opportunities to explore their favorite subjects, as Erin's days and nights were consistently overloaded. The world was too much with him; but, come September, off he went to the halls of learning.

In his first year at university Erin took residence in a Catholic college. He did receive credits for the courses he had taken at Nemson, so in effect this was his second year of university, and he continued with sciences and math and English, but now he added French and German, as he longed to read some of the world's better books in the languages in which they had originally been written.

As he burrowed more and more into the older English he was fascinated to find that this language had developed from a Germanic/Gothic structuring, through an Anglo/Saxon/Norse saga impact, and on to an admixed diction from Latin/Norman/French, all this illustrated and instantiated in the works of Chaucer, the King James Bible, and on to its full bloom in the matured epitome from the hand of Shakespeare, whose genius Erin ever after considered the non-pareil of literature. Per the bard: let us not to the marriage of true minds admit impediment.

As he advanced in the transition from Dutch to English, he succumbed to the excessive devotion of the converted and became something of a perfectionist in his use of the latter language. This was underlined at one point when, at the end of some moot expression under contention, one student, on asking if such and such were really the case, was admonished by the professor's pronouncing: "Erin said so, and Erin is seldom wrong!" By the end of term quite a number of the students in related courses took to bringing their papers, essays, and other writings to him for his critiquing and review, and Leukje enjoyed discussing and sometimes protesting against, his assessments. She was usually the more relaxed and forgiving of the two, but that was all too easy from her vantage point—little accountability in either direction from the pinnacle of the invisible voice.

At the end of the sawmill summer at home before the third year, Erin and Freya were married, having arranged that they would stay in the houslet beside the big round house that his sister Ayna and in-law Murve had built near Pitfield. Luckily Freya was able to get a job as practical nurse right on the way to the university, so the two were able to leave at the same time in the morning and come back together in the evening. The money was a big help, and nicely supplemented the grants and scholarships that Erin had manoeuvred to win when he left Nemson. The dark green Volkswagen bug they had bought together when she was boarding at the farm/meat shop place before they actually set a date to wed, came in really handy now. Odd that his parents had allowed that, but Erin had already become daddytwo in many ways, so there was little fuss.

He had not told anyone about Leukje, not even Freya. It just didn't seem really necessary. In any case, how could one explain such a thing? That every now and then a child might have an invisible friend has been common knowledge forever, and it only attracts comment as an amusing diversion, the usual outcome of it being that sooner or later the phenomenon just ceases to occur. But Erin was already beyond the usual age when he first became aware of Leukje, and long before now she had become much more than just an invisible friend—she was unusual in: proclivities; independence and dependency; her own very separate consciousness; the capacity to be heard; to be visible or not. A strange case.

Do any others have such an enduring companion, one whom could even be called spiritual? But surely the invisible friend syndrome, if one can call it that, is merely a psychological set of trials in experimentally developing one's own firmer self? Any sighting and any sounding would be hallucinative, a rebounded and a reflexive imagining. And finding in such a construct a separate will is at the very least contentious. How does she go so far afield, finding things to teach him, inform him of, even admonish him about. Does she take some part of him along?

He cannot just be dreaming when these things happen. If he were, he would himself be making the observations which, as it is, she reports to him as if relating things new to both of them. From nearby, from far away, it matters not.

Erin has started to read and collect some of the better occult books, and he finds a whole group of them having to do with Edgar Cayce. What a fascinating case it was. There is a large building dedicated to housing, studying, interpreting, and teaching all the readings this good man gave, the vast majority of which had been prompted by people with physical, even with psychological difficulties, contacting him, which in most cases he was more than helpful in resolving. Again poor Erin ponders those things undreamt of, and as he must, he dreams of them.

A point of interest about Cayce—in his adult life he read the bible cover to cover once per year. Fundamentalist? Certainly not in any usual sense, for such a person would have nothing to do with psychic readings of any sort, let alone perform them himself to the point of exhaustion, and that for the sake of persons who as often as not were indifferent, or even opposed to, religion. And a phone call or letter was enough—all he needed was a location so he could, in trance, find the person, not having heard of or seen him before that initial contact. An instance of psychic traveling before a little joke Leukje had ever been conceived.

Erin's inveterate reading in ever widening areas has led him to pull back somewhat in the courses he was taking. He has decided to take combined honors in English and French, and terminate his formal studies in the sciences. But of course there are aspects of the softer sciences that still motivate his more private searching, and he continues to pursue questions of cosmogony, cryptozoology, human evolution, psychology, the occult, and philosophy, with his wonted gusto.

But practical matters have started coming to the fore, restricting his scope. By the time he graduates, he and Freya have two sons, and her health has suffered. Their summers had switched between his working at plywood mill construction locally with Murve, and at sawing in ShallowsArc. He was a sawyer now. Time for some planning. He is not committed to any goal, for now he's divided between working on his MA and getting a teaching certificate. It's decided he should work at both until a better focus emerges, so in his fifth year he takes some courses towards the MA, and some towards high school teaching, while himself teaching first year philosophy, and first year English language and literature.

Another twist arises. At the end of his presenting a seminar paper on the psychology of adolescence the head of psychology takes him aside and suggests he should stay on as professor, and do work in the philosophy of psychology!

# Chapter 3

## A Revelation Before

It would have been the King James that southern baptist Cayce was reading yearly, almost certainly, though an acolyte of Roman bent would have turned to the Douay-Rheims, or even the Vulgate, or more recently, the Jerusalem Bible. And every one of them colored slanted and shaped by the beliefs of the mind that tried, according to its most cherished convictions, to just slightly improve on the before, to yield a definitely more fitting, compassionate and more exact, after.

Erin had been the editor of the church bulletin before Ron came along, and the two together more or less drifted into joint editorship of the high school paper. They had also competed in essay contests, as often as not sharing first prize. At university Erin had been active in writing as well, a notable feat at the end of a course in Shakespeare was his writing the exam in the Elizabethan vernacular, which apparently had never been done before, according to the professor. First class, Erin, first class. But then, 'never' is such a long and careless word.

In ShallowsArc he had explored local churches and religious groups, and noticed that the less of old history had passed in forming any church persuasion, the more a literal and word for word interpretation of revelation was the norm. Interesting situation, that—another instance of that passion of the converted?

Leukje had little to contribute in this regard, as she was typically behind Erin in this sort of speculation about theory, generally simply following his lead. When Erin first brought up the idea of infallibility she could hardly fit it in with any of her experience, though after a few discussions she grasped it in concept but was hard pressed to see how it would obtain in the real world as she could see it.

They agreed that revelation likely was a type of communication that would in the scheme of things be almost always in process somewhere or other, and not untypically, using states such as lucid dreaming or incipient awakening.

Erin is a night owl, and if he goes to bed before two am he tends to lie still, eyes open, pondering the imponderables. This brings Leukje, who just sits by the bed, not waking Freya, but engaging in their silent conversation for a time.

She has told him she has met up occasionally with what seem to be angels, but she cannot be sure, as there has been no communication, just glimpses and glances—shimmering ships passing in the mists of unsupporting night. Each time she was intrigued and hoped for more, while afraid what the more might be.

One day: "Erin, I have met with two of them." He knows what she means. "And what are they? Are they angels?" She: "I asked them, but they said they are reciters, one of them sounded as if he was reading aloud, and the other one commented on what the first one had said, although what she said also seemed to be from some sort of script." Erin: "He and she? Were they holding anything, like a paper or a book?" "No, they either looked at me or else just up a bit, as if they were, well, reciting." He, "Like a priest, saying the mass?" Leukje "No, not automatic, not really preformed. More like doing translation, in real time."

He "So what were they saying? Do you remember any of it?" "No, just sort of an impression. But they did speak to me directly at the end—they said they were going to train me, teach me to more or less record what they would say. I asked them why, and you know what they said?" "Well, what?" "They said they would do this so I could teach you." "Me? What can they know about me?"

Leukje, "I have no idea. I never mentioned you. They did. So they must be like angels." He, "Yeah. So what did they look like?" She, "Like people, actually, but it was hard to make out any detail because they gave off a soft gentle light, all around them." "Were you in a building or a room?" "No, more like a clearing in the woods, and we sat at some kind of table with a bench around it." Erin "Was it daylight? Did they have wings?" Leukje, "Oh, you're so silly. I told you they looked like people. And the light was that of early evening. But look, for now that's enough. You should get some sleep or you'll be dragging your ass all day tomorrow." "Right, good night. Right." But he did not sleep, not for a long time.

Does she sleep? How little he yet knows about her. Do invisible friends sleep? In most of the stories, such friends behave much like the children whom they hang with. But she doesn't much fit with such accounts. She has a mind, she certainly does—what about a brain? For that matter, do minds sleep? So there you go, Erin, do you think you're ready to do work in an area like the philosophy of psychology? Jackass! You better do some thinking about the real and the imagined, and in the real, you better sharpen up about classes, types, species and categories: Like which sorts of things belong together; what kind of thing just doesn't belong. Maybe you should go back to grade school. Just start over.

Check it out: why did you think Leukje is anything like what people call an invisible friend? What if she herself is some sort of semi-spiritual being? It was enough way back when she first controlled her being seen or heard, just by what would be best. The things she is now able to do are surely far beyond the scope of an invisible friend. She just has to be the sort of 'thing' they call an entity.

President Kennedy has been shot; the announcement made in psychology class. The whole world seems to be in a hubbub. How unthinkable! For such an innocent seeming figure, just summarily shot to death. There is a bigger story behind this—are things ever what they seem? And that poor lady, lord my lord.

But, time rolls on. Earth and sun keep doing steadily what they do. A hum-dinger graduation address like Erin has never heard is delivered by Northrop Frye, no less! If only a little Dutch boy could speak like that! Must get more scaffolding under him, and build and shape and build-create a higher summit. But there's no hope—flashes in a shallow pan cannot go anywhere! Bloody old hell.

Another boy, the third. Erin and Freya decide they must perforce go back to ShallowsArc and rebound to that inevitable sawmill life. Freya is so tired, chronically exhausted, and Erin too, seems to have some sort of burnout. Back to basics—the green lumber feels good to his bare hands—here is the solid and honest moil and toil that epitomizes the human condition . . . in the sweat of thy brow, thou bending beast, and the devil take the hindmost, and the hind end.

Erin starts to think there must be a medical answer to Freya's symptoms, and he reads around and comes upon a description of hypothyroidism that seems to fit the bill. They go to see the family doctor, and sure enough, he puts her on eltroxin. In about a month she starts to feel better—thank heaven for little pills!

His hands are hardened now, and even the drywood lumber strips seldom give him slivers. The body does what it must do and even hard days roll along, along.

"Erin, come on, I know you're awake. We have things to do." He "Is this some little joke, you little joke?" Leukje, "No, it is no joke, and I'm not joking. It's time we had a look at lesson one, you see, or essay one, call it what you will." "Uh-huh, and how many will there be?" "I think about two hundred." He, "What? Are you kidding? How the hell can we do that? How big is a lesson? How long is all this going to take?" "It will take quite a while, but I'm not going anywhere, and neither are you, and nothing will be lost as we go, because we will always have access later on to what we covered before." "Really? How?" Leukje, "Why don't you just relax a bit and let me give you some background, okay?" He "Alright."

Leukje "We've had some discussion about how the Judeo Christian religions first developed, beginning with the gathering together of folk tales about the early history of semitic tribes, first in oral form, and later written down, and how these were added to with the teachings of leaders of the Hebrew people, prophets and seers and with the incantations of holy men of various stripes, some more veridical and some less. One thing that distinguished this tradition from that of other peoples, was the quite early drift from polytheism to monotheism, the belief that there is one god rather than many, favoring one people, and so this group of people came to accept that they had a special place or position, distinct from any other, that Yahweh was the only true god and had chosen them to be his people.

"We often talked, too, about how revelation has occurred, often to do with some special sort of consciousness, more mystical and less rational, frequently some kind of transport into a special state or place, in short, a psychic event."

Erin "So how is one to know if what comes through is revelation, or the delusion/hallucination we associate with such states?" Leukje "How soon you forget; typical of the positivistic bent of our western society. There are three ways to evaluate or verify what comes to us by way of psychic means: the first and most general, is whether or not it makes sense, and that, of course, has a lot to do with how it compares with what we already believe to be true; the second is a bit more abstruse, and that is how it 'feels' or what is our impression of what is coming to us this way; the third is the extent to which it fits with what we know at the time or later discover to be the case—you might say how scientific it is."

He "Right, that's about how it works. I remember with Cayce the test was mostly of the first, and then the third kind, that would work the best. But he had the best results when the material was more immediately medical and for the benefit of some suffering person—it was less fruitful in more remote or esoteric subjects. And it was worst when it had anything to do with money or profit."

Leukje "You got it. We should remember that with him the fundamental motivation was healing, so the less the reading had to do with that, the less reliable the outcome tended to be. But the most important thing to remember with Cayce is that in a lot of cases he was, as near as we can tell, consulting some sort of record which itself was a transcription of already researched material; you might almost say, the result of science already done, or garnered in some way."

Erin "Gets a bit complicated, doesn't it? Almost as if there were some kind of filtering which gave him best access in questions of healing, and worst in matters that were furthest from his calling, or maybe from his knowledge otherwise.

"But we know from this case that access to some kind of record is not only logically conceivable but has been known to occur—and if we know of one, there must be others. Also I bet that in any particular case the ignition/motivation could be from either side, terra firma or otherwise." Leukje "Yes, that must be so almost from definition: before human beings were smart enough to seek revelation, the many possible sources of it were smart enough to know that the silly walking sausages were in need of some." Erin "Right on! Reminds me of that line from Star Trek, when the crystalline gritty critters described people as 'ugly bags of mostly water.' And thus we come to our present circumstance—you are about to launch us into some sort of revelatory adventure, here, now, just the two of us."

Leukje "Well, that will have to wait, your world is pressing for attention to matters more mundane like your job, your young family, your state of mind and body . . . You must get some rest, some sleep. Do some meditating, maybe. Good night, sweet prince, good night." Erin "Good night, Leukje. By the way: do you sleep? Do you meditate, or rest? Do you eat or revive your energies some other way? Do you have some attendant head butler type, a Leukje of your own?"

But she is gone—she is not here. Is she at all, anywhere? Does she have a different world that she must care for or about, at the right and fitting time(s)? We know for sure by now that she's not part of me; it is not I who thinks her—is it some other entity, thinking her into being? Or is it she herself who is an angel?

They're cutting railroad ties at the mill, mostly yellow pine, i.e. Ponderosa Pine, and the logs are in most cases big enough for number ones, measuring eight by nine inches by eight feet. Terribly heavy—a crew of men in the yard just by the sawdust pile on the far side of the mill, away from the highway, are piling them up into forklift stacks, and it takes two men to lift one, if done carefully.

There's a makeshift slide of two beams, and it's Erin's job to carry each tie across twelve feet of deck and let it drop so it slides nice and square to where the guys can get hold of it. Hard work in this hot weather. Too bad he's not sawing.

The bigger logs will make two ties, and when this happens the sawyer takes a slab and a two inch slice off opposite sides, flips it so that two would-be ties end up sitting one on the other, both still uncut for separation at the far end. The sawyer, using hydraulic levers, slides them onto spinning rollers which run the two towards the edgerman, who raises a flat iron to stop them so he can pry them apart and send them, one at a time, to where Erin can scoop each up and drop it off the deck to slide away. But here's the kicker— it happens that the edgerman is distracted, and the two-tie bundle, still stuck together, is heading right for Erin.

What can he do? Can he flip them off the rollers somehow? No, too fast, the momentum is too great. If he tries it from the far end he could not hold them back enough to tip them, and if he tries if from the receiving end he would get butted, clobbered properly and get hurt for sure, probably damage the floor as well. If he doesn't get them off there, they will go right into the burner and goodbye Charly.

He's got to grab them as if there were only one! He'll break his back. Maybe if he keeps really straight, and sort of dives across the twelve feet? No, straight and dive don't go together. No time to think—just grab the buggers. They're all watching. He grabs them, and, staggering, shuffles over to the slide and lets go.

Nobody hurt. He's a hero! And from that moment on, they call him Tarzan.

"Hello Erin. Are you ready now to explore a bit more background? Last time we sort of got stuck on Cayce, and in comparison I fear he's small potatoes. And while I think of it, no I'm not an angel. And what's more, I still do not know 'what sort of creature' I really am. And I do not understand why that is such an issue for you—when you encounter someone in a dream, do you get all exercised to know 'what sort of creature' you're dealing with? I expect not. So here's a suggestion; why don't we change my name to Lieu?—that should help, right? I will be Lieu in lieu of Leukje. Okay? You be Tarzan, and I will be Lieu, pronounce it Lew."

Erin "Okay, if you want that. Seems a silly game, to me. Why don't you try to pick up two number one yellow pine ties, and see how you dew, Lieu?"

Lieu "Now who's playing a silly game? I am trying to help you!" He "Okay, okay—I'm sorry. I'm just trying to understand you, you know? So, carry on, nurse Lieu. Just carry on and do your thing, and I'll tag along the best I can."

Lieu "Okay. Infallible scripture—just a quick glimpse: we well know that the vast majority of scripture, especially as first discovered, does not read like any sort of dictation from above, from a divine source. As a matter of fact, there's not the slightest hint that the recording mind/hand even suspects it to be inspired."

Lieu "On further reflection, on reading some revelations such as the New Testament one cannot avoid the impression that the writer, as often as not, has no idea that what he inscribes might someday be considered a part of Holy Scripture, strange as that might seem to fundamentalist devotees. But we must be clear: the fact that the mediating mind of man has no sense of divinity, or of the fact that the material which comes through may possibly be of superhuman origin, does not at all mean that it is not. Man cannot be the judge in such a case, he is too close—it will most likely be subject to a further and definitive revelation in the fullness of time, as they say. For the nonce, it is good news, 'GoodSpell."

"Okay, we should get at what I had just an inkling of when I came back and told you about the two reciters whom I encountered in that clearing at twilight. It concerns a revelation which took about 25 years to complete, and it was made to one person, a person who had been trained to receive in somewhat the same way that those two have started to train me, so I could convey what they indite, to you. But in his case the outcome will be conveyed to all who are moved to receive it. These things are not always straightforward and pedestrian—think of the maxim 'when the student is ready the master will appear.' It was so: he also serves."

"I mentioned there are about 200 essays, a lot of material, and what is revealed describes a reality much, much larger, more complex, more detailed and intricate, than anything we have imagined; as you might expect, given the time it took to transmit it all. And actually, it is pointed out time and again that only such things as may be of use to us are given. If printed, the lessons would average about ten pages each, and each is indited by an entity who is best qualified to do so, given the material covered therein. For each session I will try to bring about the amount I hope we will have time to work through with some comprehension."

"One more thing—I cannot undertake to cover everything in each essay; I hope only to deal with the main points, so we may understand them as we go."

Erin, "What about language? You mentioned those two entities seemed to be translating as they went, so if they were, what language was being translated?"

"I do not know, and I just said it seemed as if that's what they were doing; they could have been 'translating, or redacting' difficult material into a more acceptable form. For that matter, they could have been doing both. It would be most surprising if they spoke in any language at all resembling ours. In any case, all we need to know is that they put the result in the form of our English."

"Another unique angle—this revelation was not just handed down from on high in holus bolus fashion; no, there were meetings of interested people who came with all kinds of questions, and the questions were put to the person who was trained to speak aright, both in delivery and in voicing supplicant requests. So the whole process, you see, was interactive—an intricate conversation."

"No, that's not quite correct. In a conversation a question is followed right away by a response, and that's not how it went. The questions went out as inputs, and the readings that followed took those questions under advisement, but were not even mentioned in the resulting material. Quite a complicated transaction."

# Chapter 4

## Silent upon a Peak

Erin "Lieu, you said there were people involved in that revelation other than the speaker giving the delivery, the person supervising the session, the person recording the material—and a whole bunch of others who came with questions they had some interest in getting answers to. So with all that going on, how come it's not common knowledge who and where and when all this was happening? Or is it known, but just not many people have bothered about it?"

Lieu "That's a really good question, and I've been tossing that around in my head for quite a while too. The way I see it is thus: the readings that came out of this, as they were shared with all those people, were so sensible, so convincing, and so authentic, that they were accepted without serious query, and led to a spontaneous adoption, with the cooperation that ensued. Everyone was asked to keep the whole thing under wraps, especially the identity of the speaker. And that is how it has been ever since. The truest conspirator is always the happy one."

Lieu "Well, we've set the stage; we must get on and at it. In the beginning was the word, as that must be, and this is where our trip begins. 'Your world, your planet earth, and the solar system in which it spins, is part of a local universe (not to be confused with what might be termed a generic or all encompassing universe supposedly comprising all of reality,) which enfolds some ten million other such worlds—what in

Star Trek they call class M planets, fit for housing beings such as we are, more or less.

"This local universe, in turn, is part of a superuniverse, one of seven similar groupings which forms the occupancy area for 100,000 local universes similar to ours. It is a stupendous area, and it encircles, as it rotates, a central universe, of which more later. For now just remember that the central universe is where God the Father, God the Son, and God the Spirit do permanently 'reside,' if that word may be allowed to roughly indicate their 'presence,' as they are beyond residing."

Lieu "As we address mortal and finite minds we are constrained to heed the corresponding limitations, and express as sequential some transactions which, since they occurred in eternity, before time began, were judged, more exactly, coterminous. We begin, then, with God the Father's creation of God the Son and, as an objective correlative, at the same 'instant,' of Paradise. In some way not readily understandable by the minds of time and space, this same transaction involved the realization of personality by the Father, inasmuch as he achieved the relation of father to son. 'Since then' the Father is the origin of all personality."

"The Isle of Paradise is an elliptoid body of almost inexpressible size, it being greater than the total mass of all the otherwise existent reality we referenced above, inclusive of the seven superuniverses and the developing and eventuating universes of outer space. This needs be the case, since paradise is the source of the gravity forces which originate, sustain and govern the stable equilibrium of all matter in existence. All forms of reality, material, mindal, and spiritual, past, present, and future, share paradise as the place of origin, function, and destiny. Paradise is further unique in being the only entity with an absolute and totally immovable location; it is the primal center of all, and has no relation to space, either generally or specifically—it is beyond space, and it is beyond time."

"The second movement, for want of a better term, in logical but not actual sequence, was the creation, by the Father, the Son, and Paradise, of God the Spirit and the objective correlative in relation thereto, the central, perfect and already occupied by eternal and perfect inhabitants, universe of a billion worlds, which encircles paradise much as if paradise were its anchoring sun."

"What must be kept in even the matterbound mind of man, is that all the eternals alluded to in this essay thus far redacted, were, will be, are, in and from eternity, absolutely coterminous in 'origin' and 'destiny,' above/outside of time."

Erin "You are stretching my categories, Lieu, and making mincemeat of some of the concepts which I prefer to have in stable focus, hale and whole."

She "I did not say this would be easy, philosopher Tarzan. On the contrary, I indicated that the reality expounded in this revelation would be complex and astoundingly vast; if I recall aright, stupendous. I'm sorry you reel a little. I did. And too, we agreed we could go over it as often and as deeply as you wish to."

"Now, to proceed. We need a few definitions.

1. Man's body: an electro-chemical mechanism of animal origin.

2. Man's mind: a thinking, perceiving, and feeling complex giving us conscious and unconscious experience. Mind is organizer and builder, as it intervenes between spirit and matter.

3. Man's spirit: the divine spirit that indwells the mind of man; it is immortal and prepersonal though it is, if all goes well, slated to fuse with the human personality.

4. Man's soul: an experiential development from the indwelling spirit and the human mind, the nature of it is not material, and it is not spiritual—it is morontial, a state of existence between those two.

5. Man's personality: the one changeless reality in human experience that unifies all other factors of the individual human complex; a unique bestowal of God the Father, slated to survive with the human soul."

Lieu "This first section, or the selected material therefrom which we have just set forth, was indited by a divine counselor, the one in command of this whole operation. As to the language question, near the end of this first session, the point is made that 'We may resort to pure revelation only when the concept of presentation has had no adequate previous expression by the human mind'."

Erin "Well organized, from the sound of that. And think, the implication as to the breadth, scope, and detail that must be on hand for them to comb through!"

Lieu "Boggles the mind, doesn't it? And you know, one interesting thing I noticed as the two reciters and I discussed this revelation—throughout the body of it, every once in a while there is a quote from our Bible to illustrate a point, but without any reference to chapter and verse, almost like a living thesaurus."

Freya has had another baby, the third boy—good size and weight, like the first two. The very small house they were renting from the scientology practitioner fifteen miles out of town was obviously going to be too small, so the couple has bought a country place twenty miles towards Chemlupe, 140 acres with a decent house, gravity spring water, and no hydro. About four acres cultivated hayland and the rest bush, going sharply up the mountain—the railroad cuts across on the flat, taking out twenty acres of the original quarter section. Lots of work to come, on that place—a bit like starting out as pioneers.

Lieu "Well, we must push on with Ch 4. God the Father, the First Source and Center, essentially created the Son, the Spirit, Paradise, and the central universe of perfection, but the universes of time and space are all created and organized by the Paradise corps of the Creator Sons. The local universe in which we live is the creation of his Son Michael, who in turn was created, as are all creator sons, by the Father and the Eternal Son. But keep in mind that the Spirit indwelling us mortals came directly as fragmentized from the Father on Paradise, to enable each of us, if and when we are capable thereof, to communicate with Him, if we may put it thus, on a direct and private line."

"In the same way that Paradise needs be greater than the sum total of all the universes, so God needs be, as is illustrated by his ubiquity, or everywhereness, greater than all of creation, and since he is pure spirit, by his interpenetration of all things and all beings. Only from absolute infinity could he be comprehended."

"The fact of God's presence in specific mortal minds hinges on the fragment mentioned above, being there; the effectiveness of that presence is limited by the actual cooperation accorded by the mind so indwelt with that spirit spark."

"Through human history it has appeared, on occasion, that by God's fiat natural laws have been suspended, transmogrified, even reversed, to somehow alleviate a particular difficulty human beings were suffering, but the interpretation of those events were myopic—God does not do such things. His laws are eternal, and nature's laws are not bandied about in response to human supplication. This misapprehension is just another instance of man's overweening pride, or hubris."

Lieu "God's actions are all purposeful, intelligent, wise, kind, and eternally considerate of the greatest good, calibrated for the best possible outcomes for the ultimate benefits in the widest, deepest, and all encompassing blessings."

"We must beware of getting caught in any kind of corner because of our use of mathematical language. For instance when we are told, in this revelation (and or others) that although the creation of every new (local) universe requires a new adjustment of gravity, this occasions no problematical difficulty in the capacity or the potential of either God nor of Paradise (the source of gravity), and that even if an infinite increase in such creations should take place, both God and Paradise would cope without hindrance—we would have to substitute, in the implicit ever balanced equations, a symbol referencing the humanly unknown element. To illustrate, it is fairly obvious that one infinity plus one infinity equals one infinity, and the mind of man just cannot cope with that sort of 'nonsense'."

"This same rubric, of course, would apply to both spirit gravity and the source and distribution of mind, cosmic or otherwise, of which more later."

"A further caveat in respect of these conundrums: in the usual sequence of transactions, the Father delegates much to his many Sons, Creator Sons and other orders of Sons, and hence to the personalities subordinate to those orders of Sons. The Father rules through his Sons and their subordinates, right down to the Planetary Princes of the evolutionary planets—again, of which more later."

Erin "We're starting a major enterprise here, aren't we?"

She "Oh, yes. But don't worry; it's all nicely progressive, and well organized."

He "You've seen it all already?" Lieu, "No, silly. I'm just passing on to you the assurances the reciters have given me. Here's something that might help:

'1. Is <u>courage</u> good? Then man must cope with hardships, disappointments.
'2. Is <u>altruism</u> good? Then man must face serious social inequalities.
'3. Is <u>hope</u> good? Then we must deal with insecurities and uncertainties.
'4. Is <u>faith</u> good? Then let there be knowledge that falls far short of belief.

'5. Is <u>love of truth</u> good? Then we must handle errors and falsehoods.

'6. Is <u>idealism</u> good? Then let there be failings, to inspire towards the better.

'7. Is <u>loyalty</u> good? Then we must deal with betrayal and desertions.

'8. Is <u>unselfishness</u> good? Then we must long suffer the false god of the self.

'9. Is <u>pleasure</u> good? Then let there be pain and suffering all about, always.

'10. Is <u>choosing rightly</u> good? Then we need a temptation to choose wrongly.

"The perfect creatures of the central universe do not face these hardships, but they were created fully formed and beyond improvement, and thus deserve no extraordinary credit. They are fated to serve as models of perfection whenever and wherever new inhabitants of other shores will in time be contemplated."

"This was also presented by a divine counselor, one different from the first in respect of having a closer familiarity with God the Father."

Lieu "We must carry on. Some mind-blind creatures of evolutionary races have convinced themselves that god is finished with his creations, that he has withdrawn therefrom, leaving it all to its fate as though it were a dumb machine."

"It is not so. If God should retire from being the upholder of all creation, there would be an immediate and universal collapse; creation was not wound up like a clock to run just so long, to then expire and decompose—the Father unceasingly pours forth energy, light, and life. 'He stretches his hands out over empty space and hangs the earth upon nothing'." Erin "There's poetry in them thar hills."

Lieu "Oh, yes. A lofty thought in lofty language makes and takes special place and special status. 'The music of the spheres' is itself born of poetry."

'Swinging over to the opposite extreme, the eternal God is incapable of wrath and anger—such aberrations of feeling are mean and despicable, hardly fit to be called human, much less divine. This is not to say that sin will escape justice, but the results of evil are not shot forth from a weapon raised in hate—they are rather an inevitable completion of a cyclic growth of evil, resulting in an almost automatic fulfillment of a course that can only end in annihilation."

Erin "I don't understand. What about Dante's inferno, perdition, hades, hell and all that stuff?" Lieu "No, sorry to disappoint. It's not quite right to say that priests have dreamed up all that, but it was the primitive, the early tribal gods that were at the bottom of it—so, since those gods were created by the fears of men, the whole idea of eternal punishment (and how unworthy of any decent god such a notion is, I need hardly tell you) is little more than a mixture of the anguish of exaggerated guilt, and a paroxysm of unnatural fear. A psychological parallel to it you might find in shell shock, post traumatic stress disorder, that kind of thing."

Erin "Well, if there's no hell, what happens? What are the wages of sin?"

Lieu "First of all, every sinner is given abundant opportunity to mend his ways. If he proves terminally beyond redemption, he is simply snuffed out, totally annihilated; he ends up as though he had never existed. Poof! Mind you, there is what we would call a trial—this matter is not taken lightly. It results in a verdict."

"We must not forget either, that an actual fragment of the living God resides within the intellect of every normal-minded and morally conscious mortal. So it stands to reason that if the erring space-time creature has even a tiny willingness to heed the soft voice within, it is there for him to heed. Think back to when we spoke of one of the tests in determining if a revelation is genuine—we should have access to a reaction plus or minus from the godspark to guide us. All we need to do is to be open to it, to listen for it. He does much more than meet us halfway; he comes right into us, and is intimately associated with our nascent soul and our spiritualizing self. How could one possible ask for more?"

"And we must accept also that neither poverty nor any other impairment of normal opportunities for development of self, as in lack of education, supportive kith and kin, any sociomoral differentials whatsoever, would be adequate excuse for the simple matter of not listening. There simply is no acceptable reason for anyone's not choosing to embark on the journey to the portals of Paradise."

# Chapter 5

## The Inward Path

Lieu "The preceding was, again, by a divine counselor. Henceforth I will point out it is other than such a counselor. And now we start on Ch 5"

"The fact that vast time passes in the attainment of God should not perturb anyone—the time is not oppressive, not onerous, for though you swing around the circuit of the seven superuniverses, you may expect, in spirit and in status, to be ever swinging inward, to be translated from sphere to sphere in your path to the innermost center of all things, on Paradise."

Lieu "Personality and spiritspark come only from the Father. Personality is one of the great mysteries; it is potential in all mind endowed creatures, even those of minimum self-consciousness. It is not a progressive achievement; there either is or is not personality, and it is self-determinative and self-creative." Erin "It, too, seems to be a divine spark." Lieu "Yes, you're right. God provides for the sovereign choice of all true personalities; the eternity portal opens only in response to personal free choice."

"To the children of a local universe, the Creator Son or Michael Son is, to all practical intents and purposes, God, but there is only one First Source Father. The Eternal Son is the spiritual personalization of divine reality, unqualified spirit, and absolute personality, who as Second Source Son, is coordinately eternal with the Father. As the Second Person

43

of Deity, he is the original and only-begotten Son of God and ever has been and ever will be, the living and divine Word."

"The Father loves his universe children as a father; the Eternal Son looks upon all creatures both as a father and as a brother. He is first a cocreator and then a spiritual administrator as well as the Personality Absolute."

Lieu "In the same sense that God is the Universal Father, the Son is the Universal Mother, and all of us, high and low, constitute their universal family."

"In the same way that Paradise, the objective correlative of the Eternal Son, controls all physical gravity, the Son controls all spiritual gravity, and strange as it may seem 'celestial scientists' are able to calculate and calibrate spiritual circuits and powers in much the same way as our astronomers do local gravity."

"The gravity control of spiritual things operates independently of time and space, so that spirit energy is transmitted without diminution by physical gravity or distance, although the qualitative value of spirit does affect responsiveness, and every time a spiritual reality actualizes in the universes there is an immediate and instantaneous adjustment of spirit gravity." Erin "And you think I'm going to remember all this, just from one hearing?" Leu "As I said, we can reiterate later."

"An interesting corollary: spirit gravity also operates between individuals and groups of them—the term 'kindred spirits' can be more than a figure of speech, and the expression 'soul-mates' can indicate much more than mere poetic fancy."

"You have come across the dictum 'Let us make man in our own image.' And now you know this refers to the Father sending his spirit fragment as well as the gift of personality to the mortals of earth (and the creatures of billions of other such planets), so they may enter the divine plan of progressive attainment unto the portals of Paradise itself, and graduate onward to become spirit perfect."

"Part two of this plan involves the bestowal of Paradise Sons to rehabilitate the perfection enterprise in cases where misguided creatures have abused the free will given them and compromised the divine perfection project. This was seen to occur in earth's redemption from the worst of the effects of Lucifer's rebellion, by way of the bestowal of the Creator Son, Christ Michael."

"Part three is the ministry of mercy, in which the third person of the Trinity plays a special role as the conjoint executive of the Father and the Son. Thus do the Deities cooperate in the work of creation, evolution, revelation, restoration, and compassionate ministration to promote the directive 'Be you perfect'."

"Every time the Father and the Eternal Son jointly project a new, original, and absolute personal thought, that very instant this creative idea is perfectly and finally personalized in the being and personality of a new, original Creator Son, who will go forth and with the cooperation of the Third Source and Center, complete the organization of a time-space universe of progressive evolution."

"Magisterial Sons are personalized jointly by the Son and the Spirit—these Sons will serve as judges of survival in the creations of time and space."

"The Father, Son, and Spirit, as Trinity, unite to personalize the Trinity Teacher Sons, who perform teaching services to all personalities, human and divine."

"All Sons of God who take origin in the persons of the three Deities are in direct and constant communication with the Eternal Mother Son, an instant communication not affected by time, though at times subject in part to space."

Lieu "The very instant that the Father and the Son conjointly conceive an identical and infinite action, God the Infinite Spirit springs into replete existence."

"The God of Action functions and the dead vaults of space are astir—one billion perfect spheres flash into existence where no material reality obtained a moment before, and in that very instant gravity is enactively in force, outflowing spirit and creature personality encharges organized space, and thus is prepared the very soil of life for the consciousness of mind in the associated intelligence circuits of the Infinite Spirit. There is no record of all this as such, but the Spirit has verified the fact that the central universe and all that pertains to it eternalized simultaneously with his attainment of personality and consciousness of being."

"The Third Person deitizes by this very act of conjoint creation, and he thus forever becomes the Conjoint Creator. We thus portray the origin of the Third Source and Center as an interpretative condescension to the time-bound and space-conditioned minds of mortal creatures—a parable to part-understanding."

"The Eternal Son and the Conjoint Creator have, as partners and through their coordinate personalities, planned and fashioned every post-center time space universe that has taken its place in one of the superuniverses since the very beginning of time. A Creator Son of the Eternal Son, and a Creative Spirit of the Infinite Spirit have created you and your universe, and it devolves upon them to foster and sustain this work and to minister to the creatures of their making. There will be more detail concerning these matters as our narrative unfolds."

"As the Son conveys and makes real the love of the Father, the Spirit in his ministry brings forth and gives expression to the mercy of the Son. In the local creations the Spirit does not come down to the material races in the likeness of mortal flesh as do certain of the Sons of God, but the Spirit and his coordinate Spirits do downstep themselves in a series of attenuations, until they can appear as angels to stand by your side and guide you in your lowly earthly existence."

"The Spirit is endowed with absolute mind and as such is the source of the endowment of intellect throughout the universes. He is the god of mind and of matter and he is a person, a merciful one, who has unique prerogatives of energy control. The agencies of the Conjoint Actor ceaselessly manipulate the forces and energies of all space. The Conjoint Creator consistently functions in consonance with and in recognition of, the material absoluteness of Paradise."

"The providence of God is the domain of the Conjoint Creator; no actual or actualizing reality can escape eventual relationship with the Third Source and Center. He functions specifically wherever energy and spirit interact; dominates all reactions with mind; and exerts a mighty influence over mind and matter."

"A point of note: The Spirit is actually omnipotent only in the domain of mind; herein his sovereignty is unqualified—in all else he shares with Father and Son."

"The universe of your origin is being forged between the anvil of justice and the hammer of suffering, but those who wield the hammer are the children of mercy, the spirit offspring of the Infinite Spirit." Erin "That makes me just a bit uncomfortable—brings to mind the idea of tough love. Is that implicit here?"

Lieu "It does sound that way, yes. But you must remember that expressing the concepts and the reasoning underlying this revelation in our earth anchored English language must be very awkward for these divine counselors, so we will forgive their occasionally resorting to indirect and sometime picturesque speech as they work their 'translation,' and this may well be an instance where they did not get it quite right. Or possibly we're not getting the right idea in this case."

Erin "I suppose. Excuses, excuses. They should let us participate somehow."

Lieu "Can't imagine how. This is pretty much one way, you know—not an interactive group think—more like dictation. We just have to make the best of it."

Erin "Yes, of course. I'm just getting a bit tired, going into overload. Anyway, carry on nurse, do your thing and it will all come good with the next wash."

Lieu "Okay then, on with the mind and matter mother. The Infinite Spirit has a unique power, that of antigravity, and it is transmissible to certain of her daughter personalities. This power annuls physical gravity within a local frame, and that is done by an opposing force presence. In similar vein a power of neutralizing energy comes into the picture, and this is done partly by slowing down energy to the point of materialization. Remember that the Conjoint Creator is not the source of energy but rather the manipulator of it, working through: physical controllers; power directors; power centers, and other unrevealed aides which come into play on occasion. Not so straightforward as we might hope."

"Paradise is the pattern of infinity and its material fulcrum; the agencies of the Third Source are the levers which motivate the material level of existence and inject spontaneity into the mechanisms of the physical creations."

"The mind endowment of the seven superuniverses is derived from the Seven Master Spirits, the primary personalities of the Conjoint Creator, each distributing cosmic mind to the corresponding superuniverse; the First to number One, the Fourth to number Four, and so on. Cosmic mind is conditioned by time, and as descent is made from the infinite to the adjutant levels of mind, intellect must increasingly reckon with the limitations of space. Even the Father fragments need the preparation for their encouchment in the minds of evolutionary creatures that is provided by the Spirit, and the very possibility of a lowlevel mind is ensured for the more primitive nonexperiencing living beings. Note that human intellect is rooted in the material origin of animal races. The planetary life on earth is one."

"Although your minds are destined to divine dignity, too often you mar them by insincerity, subject them to animal fear and distort them by useless anxiety. The contemplation of the immature and inactive human intellect should only lead to humility. Take note that as the Father draws and centers all personality, the Son permeates all spirit, and so the Spirit exercises an overcontrol of all mind."

"Mind gravity can operate independently of material and spiritual gravity, but when the latter two impinge, mind gravity always functions. Mind, even in the case of impersonal beings, qualifies them to think and thus gives them their consciousness, despite the total absence of personality."

Erin "Consciousness in the absence of personality—that seems like a bit of a stretch, don't you think." Lieu "Perhaps we need to review what we understand by 'consciousness.' Most people believe that when they work at solving some difficulty or problem, their awareness follows along every step of the way, and this, actually, is an illusion. The thinking part does not take place in awareness; it is a black box activity, and awareness or consciousness does not obtain until the results of the thinking emerge and are on hand for classifying, categorizing, and cataloguing in the memory banks. But you know all this—you've read Julian Jaynes, and you haven't relinquished what you learned there, have you?"

Erin "No, not at all. Guess I skipped over a small gap in what seemed like an immediate connection between 'think' and 'consciousness,' which was implied."

She "Good, that's cleared up, then. Maybe you should browse through *"The Origin of Consciousness in the Breakdown of the Bicameral Mind"* again—clumsy and unfortunate title though it was, it's still a bloody good piece of work."

Erin "Your diction is losing its angelic luster." Lieu "Up your nose. Now, we need to look at another wrinkle in this maze of fabric. The Conjoint Actor, as that title implies, coordinates all actuality by simultaneously recognizing the material, the mental, and the spiritual and can, moreover, focus all that at any given point. This is called 'universe reflectivity.' It is especially well shown on each of the architectural headquarter worlds of the seven superuniverses, as it enables the universe rulers to know about remote conditions simultaneously, as they arise."

"There are seven Reflective Spirits at the capital of each superuniverse, and it is by acting through these that the Seven Master Spirits effectively govern."

"Every time the Father and the Eternal Son enparent a Creator Son, the Conjoint Actor provides for that Son a Creator Spirit and they two will in close association care for a local universe, and what the Infinite Spirit is to all creation, a Creative Spirit is to a local universe."

Erin and Freya have three sons and a daughter now. He still works at sawmilling, though the bush farm takes up a lot of his time. He has built a barn for the stock, with space for the winter hay in the top section, up under the shake covered roof. Just one cow gets milked, and since the goats are still doing their part, the milk from the cow is sold to a neighbor not far away. The calf is in with the goats in a huge one acre pen that he built with slabs from the mill in town.

He has worked his way up through the ranks, right up to superintendent. One day, in discussion with one of the owners, the idea comes up that he should be an accountant and take over the office, so he might establish better control over the whole operation, from the trees in the bush to the pencils in his pocket.

So now he has started taking the CMA accounting courses at a college in Chemlupe. He travels with a Mormon friend, taking turns with the driving, and they both enjoy the opportunity to have some good discussions on religion.

Erin is excused the English course, as he is better qualified than the prof.

# Chapter 6

## The Trinity

Lieu "The Universal Father has divested himself of everything that was possible to bestow on any other creator or creature; he has delegated to others all power and every authority that could be delegated, and has transferred to his Sovereign Sons, in their respective universes, all administrative authority that could be transferred. So you see, he has always given all that he could give."

Lieu "When human beings form associations, such as, say, families, or social groups, school classes, fraternities or sororities, churches, corporations, unions, professional groupings, political parties—the group potential always far exceeds the simple summation of their individual attributes and proclivities. In the same way the three deities, when united as the Trinity, form a completely new and more absolutizing creatorship than any or all of them could do in any other representation or configuration."

"The application of law, justice, falls within the province of the Paradise Trinity and is carried out by certain Sons of the Trinity. Take note that justice is never a personal matter; it is always a plural function. The group of Trinity Sons embraces the following personalities:

1. Trinitized Secrets of Supremacy
2. Eternals of Days

3.  Ancients of Days
4.  Perfections of Days
5.  Recents of Days
6.  Unions of Days
7.  Faithfuls of Days
8.  Perfectors of Wisdom
9.  Divine Counselors
10. Universal Censors

These orders represent the collective attitude of the Trinity only in the domain of executive judgment—justice. They represent the Trinity only in that specific function and mainly for it were they personalized."

"We have 'met' several Divine Counselors in their role as revelators, either as speakers or as supervisors of the ongoing presentation of these lessons."

Lieu "Paradise serves many purposes but to creatures it is primarily the dwelling place of the Father, at the very center of the upper surface. This presence of the Father is immediately surrounded by the personal presence of the Eternal Son, and they are both invested with the glory of the Infinite Spirit."

"Paradise is essentially flat, and from the upper to the lower surface is about one tenth of the diameter. The greater out-pressure of force-energy at the north end established absolute direction in the master universe; however, Paradise exists without time and has no location in space as such."

"Space seemingly originates just below nether Paradise. The Isle is made of a material that is found nowhere else in creation; it is the original nonspiritual expression of the

First Source and Center. The periphery is occupied in part by the landing and dispatching fields for various groups of spirit personalities; neither upper nor nether Paradise is approachable by transport supernaphim or other types of space traversers."

"Between Paradise and the Perfect Central Universe are three sets of seven spheres each. The outermost set is dedicated to the Infinite Spirit, and on each of them is a Master Spirit, alluded to previously, and each Master Spirit maintains force-focal headquarters, with flash stations, on the Paradise periphery, attended by one of the Seven Supreme Power Directors. This arrangement has to do with certain Paradise energies going out to each superuniverse, 3 to 3, 6 to 6, etc."

"The outer margins of the nether surface of the Isle is a vast elliptical force center; the primordial force-charge of space is apparently focalized in this area, the inside part of which is devoted to the functions of the Isle itself, and the outermost to the vast currents of charged space energy going to the outer reaches of the superuniverses, and the depleted space currents returning—note that these energies are not responsive to physical or linear gravity such as we observe, being space-time scientists, but they are to Paradise gravity, which is a very different phenomenon, unresponsive to distance/mass. For a little more than one billion earth years this space-force is outgoing, then for about the same period of time it is incoming. Do you see how nicely this answers all those pesky questions about 'the expansion of the universe,' and the anomalies in the measurements of same, and the dozens of conundrums about that ether of the modern mind:

'The Big Bang'!" Erin "Well, we should be chary of the self-congratulatory and selfindulgent temptations based on what is plainly a sort of side effectively spurious hindsight." Lieu "I suppose. But just a bit of icing.

"The assumption that the expansion has been constant in all directions has been troublesome, so that assumption has been under fire due to unexpected variations in the expansion readings. A moment of reflection can tell you why that is the case: that the expansion is one phenomenon, and that its place of origin is naturally at a center of some sort, we have just learned to be exactly what is happening, but earth is in one of the local universes on the outer edge of one of the superuniverses, so the better the telescopes we devise, the worse the reading variations become. The solution would be to take readings from Paradise."

Lieu "The universe of universes is not an infinite plane, a boundless cube, nor a limitless circle; it clearly has dimensions. The observable behavior of the material creation evinces a space unit, an organized and coordinated whole."

"The successive space levels of the master universe constitute the major divisions of pervaded space—organized and inhabited, or yet to be so. Proceeding outward from Paradise, the master universe consists of six concentric ellipses, so there are seven elements, thus:

1. Paradise
2. Central Universe
3. seven superuniverses
4. 1st outer space

5.  2$^{nd}$ outer space
6.  3$^{rd}$ outer space
7.  4$^{th}$ outer space

"Note that the first two are not time creations—they are eternal."

"Paradise is stable in and of itself and is surrounded by its 21 satellites; the central universe is enclosed by a ring of enormous dark gravity bodies, such that the mass content of all this nuclear grouping is far in excess of that embodied in the mass of the seven sectors of the grand universe: the center must keep hold."

"Note that the boundaries of the superuniverses are not geometrically precise—the borders do not cut across any organized groupings, systems, or nebulae. They are simply space clusterings of about one seventh each of the physical volume between the central universe and the outer space worlds abuilding. What we call the grand universe is the present organized and inhabited creation, i.e. the seven superuniverses—its organization and occupancy is not yet complete; it is comprised of about seven trillion inhabited planets, not including the specially constructed administrative worlds. The master universe includes the grand universe plus the as yet uninhabited outer space creations."

"It is near the outer limits of the seventh superuniverse that your planet earth is located, in a fairly new local universe, so you are in the newer portion of a by definition newer superuniverse. A Johnny come lately sort of thing."

Erin "Well, think of all the experience we should be able to access."

Lieu "I much doubt that anything so straightforward would come into play, especially if you consider that we essentially would hardly rate."

Erin "Are you just being considerate, including yourself in the 'we,' or is this a side of you that I never dreamt of?" Lieu "Well, if we're going to get poetic about it, I must point out to you that my sense of self is barely half a sense—somehow my self seems interpenetrated with yours. How's that for a puzzle?"

Erin "Oh lord, deliver us from doubt, and from any other such evils."

Lieu "Come now, Tarzan dear, it is not meet to label doubt an evil. Simply consider doubt an opportunity to redesign the scaffolding, to reach up higher."

"Avast! We must proceed. Between the outer belt of the seven superuniverses and the gigantic circuits of the first outer space cauldrons, there is a quiescent space zone shell of a thickness which averages 400,000 light years, and then begins an active shell of 25 million light years, the first outer space level, which encircles the whole of the known, organized, and inhabited creations. So, now you have some inkling of what you might call the lay of the lands beyond."

Lieu "In the near future new telescopes will reveal to earth's astronomers no less than 75 million new galaxies in outer space, so hold on. The game's afoot."

"There are four presence circuits under the aegis of the Father:

1. The personality gravity of the Father;

2. The spirit gravity of the Eternal Son;

3. The mind gravity of the Conjoint Actor; and

4. the cosmic gravity of Paradise. None of these is related to the nether Paradise force center: they do not involve force, energy, or power. As presence circuits they are independent of time and space."

"Individuals have their guardians of destiny; planets, systems, constellations, and universes have their respective rulers, who labor for the good of their domains. As to the watch care of the master universe as a whole, the Architects of the Master Universe serve in ministry, prior to the advent of specific rulers."

"Brotherhood is a fact of relationship between every personality in existence. The part profits or suffers in measure with the whole. The relative velocities of part and whole determines which is retarded or carried forward by the other. Do not make the mistake of assuming that the immensity of God interposes an unbridgeable separation between you and him—remember that he is part in you."

"Reality, measured by physical gravity response, is measured quantitatively. The mind of any personality, measured by spiritual gravity response, displays spirit content qualitatively, a measure of the living energy of divinity. Mind entails that by which spirit realities become experiential to creature personalities, and so even the human mind is supermaterial in unifying things, ideas, and values."

"There are these three things:

1. Matter—organized energy subject to linear gravity except as modified by motion or conditioned by mind.
2. Mind—an organized consciousness not wholly subject to material gravity especially as modified by spirit.
3. Spirit—the highest personal reality, not subject to linear gravity but slated to become the motivator of all evolving energy systems of personality dignity. In cosmic evolution matter becomes a shadow cast by the mind in the presence of spirit luminosity—in death both mind and spirit survive, but the body does not. Here ends this section, presented by a Perfector of Wisdom." Erin "Can you tell me something about a Perfector of Wisdom?"

Lieu "Not at this time—I expect we will come across that sometime later."

Erin "Tell me a bit more about how this works, do you sit down with those two reciters and they tell you a whole chunk, and then you just remember it?"

She "Oh no! Nothing as outward and straightforward as that. Remember how Edgar Cayce would go, while in trance, and look up what he wanted to know? Well, even that is more mundane than what has been happening with me. As far as I can tell they must be putting this into my head when I'm sleeping, because for a long time now I've neither seen them nor had any conversation with them. And when I want to give you what I've received, I just join you and start talking. It's all kind of automatic now. As far as I can tell they must have planted all that I need to say directly into my mind, my memory. I believe I can repeat what I've said to you before but I haven't tried that yet."

Lieu "As we have mentioned before, there are three circuits, each of seven special spheres, between the Isle of Paradise and the central creation."

"The innermost are dedicated to the Father, the second circuit of seven to the Eternal Son, and the outermost to the Infinite Spirit. As far as we know, they have always been there; they are eternal, like Paradise. Each world in the circuit of the Father and that of the Spirit has a distinct type of permanent citizenship, and, as mentioned before, each world of the Spirit has one of the seven Master Spirits."

"The Father's spheres are directed by the highest order of the Stationary Sons of the Trinity, the Trinitized Secrets of Supremacy. One of the spheres has to do with the rendezvous of the Father fragments; another with Sons of the Eternal Son; yet another with the foregathering of the Master Spirits and entities having to do with universe reflectivity; a fourth with trinitized beings and those with authority to represent the Trinity; a fifth is the home of Solitary Messengers and the status sphere of the Universe Power Directors; the sixth is the destiny sphere of the angelic hosts—supernaphim, seconaphim, and seraphim, and has to do with seraphic transport; and the final or seventh is the rendezvous of the ascendant creatures of space on their way to Paradise as they proceed in the development of their immortal soul and their fusion with the Father fragment."

"The Seven Master Spirits are the mind-spirit balance wheel of the grand universe as they each power direct their respective superuniverses from their dedicated Infinite Spirit spheres, though when they gather to confer they do so on the third of the Father spheres."

"From the periphery of Paradise to the inner borders of the superuniverses, occur the following conditions:

1. a ring of quiescent space
2. the clockwise processional of the twenty-one special spheres and the seven circuits of the central universe
3. the semiquiet space to the gravity bodies
4. the inner ring of counterclock circling dark gravity bodies
5. the second space zone, between the two rings of dark gravity bodies
6. the outer ring of clockwise circling dark gravity bodies
7. the third semiquiet space zone, extending to the inner ring of the seven superuniverses."

"The dark gravity bodies are unique in that they neither reflect nor absorb light, and their size, number, and distribution are such that they so completely enshroud the whole of the inner and the eternal creations that the total effect is to make this enormous kernel of centricity, from outer gravity bodies to central Paradise, totally black/invisible, even to the innermost space astronomers."

"In this second part of lesson 6 we have explored what we long ago called the objective correlative of the great initiant 'creation' of all the perfect centers. Now we need to consider the opposite, the subjective correlative aspect of the return journey, which obtains at the opposite extreme of the reality continuum in that it proceeds, not from pure spirit to meterable reality but from feet of clay to an eventual spirit existence—that is, the ascension progression from mud to God."

Lieu "On earth at birth you have already benefited from the evolutionary struggle to attain the state of being human, and from that point till death you seriously test and quest to become a being more whole, ensouled."

"On the mansion worlds, and up through your system, your constellation, and your local universe, you learn/work along the morontia phase of existence. On the training worlds of your superuniverse you learn/work unto the true spirit stages of progression, and are prepared for eventual transit to Preheaven (a convenient term in this context for the seven circuits of the central universe) where are intellectual, spiritual, and experiential tasks to be achieved on all those worlds, from the seventh to the first circuit. Each of these billion study worlds is a veritable university of surprises; monotony is not a part of the Preheaven career."

Erin "The path to Paradise is no small matter, is it? Words fail me."

Lieu "Well, I guess the words are my chore, but it's no big deal. I must be getting good help, because I need not work at it—they just come out as needed."

Erin "You might do really well at university, if you can come out with all that material as if you're sleepwalking. You think it's all recorded in your head?"

Lieu "No, that can't be because I jump into explanation or discussion with you and don't seem to lose any continuity. Right now I feel the need to review the layout of organized, inhabited reality, okay? In order of scale, here goes."

"The basic unit of supergovernment is the system, comprising some 1,000 class-m worlds, each of which normally has a Planet Prince, and the system itself has a system sovereign, ruling from a specially constructed headquarter sphere."

"Next is the constellation, comprising 100 systems, ruled from a built world by three Vorondadek Sons, and also attended by a Faithful of Days."

"Then we have a local universe, being 100 constellations, ruled from its head-quarter world by a Michael Son, and attended by a Union of Days."

"One hundred local universes make up a minor sector, so comprising a billion class-m planets, more or less, ruled over by three Recents of Days."

"The major sector holds 100 minor ones, or a 100 billion manned planets, ruled by three Perfections of Days."

"A superuniverse has 100 major sectors, sustaining one trillion class-m planets, ruled by three Ancients of Days."

"The seven superuniverses hold seven trillion manned planets, and are governed from Paradise by the Seven Master Spirits."

"Now, the seventh superuniverse, in which we live, has ten major divisions, and earth astronomers have identified eight of them, the remaining two being difficult to place as being of a piece, due to our partial immersion therein."

"A few words about suns, the stars of space: trillions of years an ordinary sun 'burns,' illustrating the amazing energy stored in each unit of matter. Certain conditions enable suns to send forth much space energy that comes their way; many phases of energy and all forms of matter are captured and distributed by these solar dynamos, as they play their part of automatic power-control stations."

Lieu "The headquarters of your local system has seven worlds of transition culture, each of which is encircled by seven satellites, among which are the seven mansion worlds, man's first post-mortal residence. As the term heaven has been used on earth it has sometimes meant these seven mansion worlds, the first one referring to the first heaven, and so on to the seventh."

"The headquarters of your constellation has seventy satellites of socializing culture and training, for candidates of ascension leaving the mansion worlds."

"The capital of your local universe is surrounded by ten university clusters of forty-nine spheres each. Here are men spiritualized after constellation lessons."

"Headquarters of your minor sector is surrounded by seven spheres of physical studies of ascendant life."

"That of your major sector, centers seventy spheres of intellectual training."

"The headquarters of your superuniverse is surrounded by seven higher universities of advanced spiritual training, and each of these seven clusters of wonder spheres consists of seventy specialized worlds containing thousands of replete institutions wherein the pilgrims of time are re-educated preparatory to their long flight to Preheaven, the Central Universe."

Erin "Does all this just go on, forever and ever, amen?" Lieu "No, there is a sort of endtime, which is called being settled in light and life. When a spiritual harmony in a local universe develops such that its spirit circuits become pretty much indistinguishable from those of the encompassing superuniverse, its physical state is in equilibrium, and it shows a universal loyalty to its Creator Son, then the local universe immediately swings into the settled circuits of light and life. Our local universe, however, has not even achieved the prime condition of physical stability. A long time need pass for all conditions to be met."

"Each superuniverse is presided over by three Ancients of Days, the joint chief executives of the supergovernment; there are seven such executives:

1.  Ancients of Days,3
2.  Perfectors of Wisdom, 1 billion
3.  Divine Counselors, 3 billion
4.  Universal Censors, 1 billion
5.  Mighty Messengers
6.  Those High in Authority
7.  Those without Name and Number

Group 2, 3, and 4 are Coordinate Trinity Personalities, and the remaining three are glorified ascendant mortals, classed as Trinitized Sons of Attainment."

"The coordinate council of a superuniverse consists of the above executives plus sector rulers and regional overseers, some previously listed, as follows:

1. Perfections of Days
2. Recents of Days
3. Unions of Days
4. Faithfuls of Days
5. Trinity Teacher Sons
6. Eternals of Days
7. Reflective Image Aids, which seven are the spokesmen of the Seven Reflective Spirits, and thus represent the Seven Master Spirits of Paradise."

"The seven superuniverses do not maintain any sort of ambassadorial representation; they are completely isolated from each other. They know of mutual affairs only through the Seven Master Spirits."

# Chapter 7

## The Power

Lieu "There is a judicial branch of government, but it does not involve specified personnel. The courts of justice are in the domain of various selected entities already introduced to you, doing special duty in that respect. A point of note: sentences involving the extinction of will creatures are finalized only on superuniverse headquarters, by the Ancients of Days. "There is no appeal from rulings by superuniverse authorities, as they are the concurred opinions of the Ancients of Days and the ruling Master Spirit." "Here ends this section, presented by a Universal Censor"

Erin and Freya have decided they should modernize their home a bit, add a few rooms, put a new roof over the back part, and put in electricity. There had been only an outhouse, thirty feet from the front of the house, just by the barn, but that was a bit onerous in the winter. So, best to start with the extra rooms.

Erin added a sitting room off the back of the kitchen, then a bathroom beside that, and a bedroom to the right of the bath. The plumbing was a bit tricky, since there had been no hot water other than what came off the water jacket in the wood burning kitchen range—supplying the bathroom sink with hot and cold would be more complicated. He decided to pre-plumb the hot from what would be a good spot for a hot water tank in a closed off corner of the sitting room.

The cold water supply would stay as it was, year round spring water, gravity fed from up the slope beside the hayfield. Not much pressure, but a smooth flow with no hiccups, and ever so clean and cool all through the year. It was cribbed in around the source, and all he had to do every few months was throw in a cup of bleach to keep the flatworms under control.

The hydro office sent out a foreman to look at access, and it was agreed that Erin would clear the trees from the top corner of the property to the house, that making the hypotenuse of where the hundred yard driveway made an upside down L past the field and to the house and barn. That way the power line would not even go over the driveway; more secure, better safety.

Lieu "The Seven Master Spirits are the primary personalities of the Infinite Spirit. In this sevenfold creative act of self-duplication the associatively inherent mathematical possibilities of three persons of Deity are exhausted, which also explains why the grand universe is in seven divisions, and the number seven is so prominent in all Trinity-source organization and administration."

"To illustrate: superuniverse one portrays the uniqueness of God the Father; two, the expression of the Eternal Son; three, the portrayal of the Infinite Spirit; four, the combined expression of the Father and the Son; five, that of the Father and the Spirit; six, the combined uniqueness of the Son and the Spirit; and seven, that of the Father, the Son, and the Spirit, all three, but not as Trinity."

"Succinctly, all of spirit reality, and its expression, comes and goes in sevens. And just to make certain you do not extrapolate beyond the correct bounds in this regard, take note that the physical as such, without ontogenous impact from spirit and without spirit involved in its fate or expression, is simply decimal."

"The seven Master Spirits are the creators of the Universe Power Directors and their associates, and they also very materially assist the Creator Sons in the work of shaping and organizing the local universes."

"Insofar as morontia substance and morontia mind, both intervening between the physical and the spiritual, bridge the gulf between mortal materiality and the advancing superuniverse realm of spiritual status, the Master Spirits play a part."

"Throughout all eternity an ascendant mortal will exhibit traits indicative of the presiding Spirit of the superuniverse of his nativity. Even in the Corps of the Finality, that being the end-goal status of ascendant pilgrims, when it is needed to portray a complete Trinity relationship to evolutionary creation, a group of seven finaliters is assembled, one from each superuniverse."

"The Master Spirits are the source of the cosmic mind, and this explains the kinship often observed between various types of mind. Kindred minds are very fraternal and inclined towards intercooperation. Human minds are sometimes observed to be running in channels of astonishing similarity and agreement."

"In all personality associations of the cosmic mind is observed what can well be called the 'reality response,' and it is this cosmic endowment that saves will creatures from becoming helpless victims of mistaken a priori assumptions in the realms of science, philosophy, and religion." Erin "We came across that when we were exploring how one might recognize a valid revelation as to its source."

Lieu "Right you are. These insights, these cosmic intuitions, are developed in the process of living; they are constitutive in the self-consciousness of reflective thinking. It is the purpose of education to develop and sharpen these innate endowments of the human mind; of civilization to express them; of life experience to realize them; of religion to ennoble them, and of personality to unify them." Erin "Now there's an all-encompassing mandate for the teacher. Kind of difficult to build into a curriculum though. Would take a lot of thought."

Lieu "Pushing on, we should spend a little time on personality. For one thing, and it would surprise many, the Father's conferring the gift of personality predates by far his later bestowal of the Father fragment."

"Creature personality is distinguished by two self-manifesting phenomena of reactive behavior: self-consciousness and associated relative free will. Self-consciousness includes the ability to recognize other personalities and connotes recognition of mind ministration and the realization of the relative independence of creative and determinative free will. At death, personality identity survives in and by the survival of the soul. Unselfish social consciousness must be, at bottom, a religious consciousness; you become conscious of man as your creature brother because you are already aware of God as your Creator Father."

"Now, we must consider the Seven Supreme Spirit Groups. The first three are children of the Trinity:

1. The Seven Master Spirits
2. The Seven Supreme Executives
3. The Reflective Spirits

The remaining four are brought into being by the Infinite Spirit and/or such of his associates as have the needed creative status:

4. The Reflective Image Aids
5. The Seven Spirits of Central Circuits
6. The Local Universe Creative Spirits
7. The Adjutant Mind-Spirits

"The Seven Master Spirits are the coordinating directors of the reference field's administrative realm, sometime directly and sometime less so."

"The Reflective Spirits are not merely transmitting agents; they are retentive personalities as well. Their offspring, the seconaphim, are also retentive, and thus everything of spiritual value is registered in duplicate, with one impression being preserved in the personal equipment of some member of the vast host of the secoraphic staff of the Reflective Spirits."

"The space range of the extra-Paradise reflectivity service is limited by the outer borders of the seven superuniverses, but within this sphere it appears to be independent not only of time and space but of all subabsolute universe circuits."

"The local universe Creative Spirits are each created in consonance with the creation of a local universe Creator Son. These spirits are resident with the Master Spirit of the relevant superuniverse until such time as the proposing Creator Son is about to leave on his space adventure to the location of his projected local universe, when the Father acknowledges the eternal union of the two creatives, who then go forth to launch the material organization scheduled."

"Upon the declaration by the creator Son of the intention to create life, the relevant Paradise spirit persons in concord ignite a 'primary eruption' in the person of the Infinite Spirit, the effect of which is to endow the creator Spirit with personality. When the creator Son successfully completes his seventh bestowal, and has accordingly claimed his local universe sovereignty, he declares, from the headquarters of the universe, the cosovereignty and equality with him, of the local universe Mother Spirit."

Lieu "The Supreme Spirit groups with the Infinite Spirit are the immediate creators of the vast creature family of the Third Source and Center. All orders of the ministering spirits spring from this association: primary supernaphim by the Infinite Spirit; secondary supernaphim by the Master Spirits; the tertiary by the Seven Spirits of the Preheaven central circuits; the mighty seconaphim of the superuniverse by the Reflective Spirits; and the all—original angelic orders of a local creation by the Creative Spirit of that creation."

"We've come across the expression Descending Sons of God earlier, but we should know something about them. Three groups are Paradise Sons, as follows:

1. Creator Sons—the Michaels
2. Magisterial Sons—the Avonals
3. Trinity Teacher Sons—the Daynals.

The other four groups are Local Universe Sons of God:

4. Melchizedek Sons
5. Vorondadek Sons
6. Lanonandek Sons
7. The Life Carriers

Vorondadek are Constellation Fathers. The Lanonandeks are System Sovereigns and also serve as Planetary Princes.

"The Magisterial Sons, though not creators in the personal sense, are closely associated with the Michaels in all their work. These Avonals are planetary ministers and judges, the magistrates of all the time-space realms. Each has an exclusive personality, and it is not unusual that they are incarnated in the likeness of mortal flesh, and sometimes are even born of mortal mothers. They serve as dispensation terminators, liberating the sleeping survivors, and will attend just prior to, until just after, the arrival of a bestowal Son. They will even themselves serve as a born of woman bestowal Avonal Son. When a Magisterial Son has experienced a replete record of ministrations it often happens that he becomes a member of the high personal council of a Creator Son."

"Earth has not been host to an Avonal Son on a magisterial mission. If the general plan of inhabited worlds had prevailed, earth would have been favored with such a mission between the days of Adam and the bestowal of Christ Michael, but as the bestowal in this case was also that of the Creator Son of the whole of the local universe, and this furthermore being his seventh or final bestowal, establishing his candidacy for coronation as the sovereign of our local universe, there was an element of dislocation in the usual progression of events."

Erin "My goodness, when Jesus said to the apostles that they might hence-forth be fishers of men, I wonder if it occurred to him that having an odd fish in the basket now and again could so drastically disrupt a later course of events."

Lieu "Quite a stretch in metaphor there, Tarzan. Just horsing around?"

He "Not I, m'lady teen, not I. Have I not always been a model of etiquette? And should not I have liberty to voice a random thought, to see where it might go?"

Lieu "Alright, already—let it be. On this earth there is a common belief that Christ Michael's bestowal was effected to influence the attitude of the Father, to atone for the sins of men vis a vis the doomsday judgment hanging over them. That is not so: the career of sevenfold bestowal is the goal of all Creator Sons."

Lieu "Some order of Paradise Son must be bestowed upon each mortal-inhabited world in order to make it possible for the Father fragments to indwell the minds of the mortals, and that cannot happen until such a Paradise Son has poured out the Spirit of Truth upon all flesh, and that, in turn, depends upon the return to universe headquarters of that Son's I completion of his bestowal on that evolving world. Every mortal world is destined to become host to a Magisterial Son on a bestowal mission, except that planet in each local universe whereon a Creator Son elects to make his mortal bestowal. So you can see, Erin, how great the odds were against Jesus favoring our little earth this way—ten million to one! It will come up again when we discuss His life with us."

Erin "So Jesus of Nazareth is the sovereign of this local universe, embracing ten million class-m planets and all the administration and governance thereof."

Lieu "Of course—you put that together just now? Where have you been?"

Erin "Sorry, I must have failed to make some key connections." Lieu "Well, all you had to do was ask. It's not that I myself have a solid hold on it all, but by some weird turn of fate when I try to explain things to you they just seem to come out of my pouty mouth in proper form and order. Ain't that grand? Ain't it great?"

He "Yeah. Pouty mouth and all. A great and universal pandect, holus bolus from one pouty little mouth. There's got to be some lack of justice in such a droll arrangement." Lieu "Ha ha ha!! You're jealous that you have to work so hard to put these things together nicely in that three pound blob of porridge inside your bony stubborn skull." He "I think it's called a brain, and if you remember our history with Ron, it's a pretty good one. Who's getting maliciously poetic now?"

Lieu "Of course, of course. I have no right to gloat over what is obviously a fortuitous situation from which I benefit, but can claim no credit for arranging."

Erin "Okay, let's have peace in our time, and try to survive this together."

Lieu "A moment now, another thought. It was no part of the mission of Jesus to atone for our sins, only to complete his sevenfold assignment to 'incarnate' as seven beings, ending with the human life as Jesus; to establish his entitlement to the sovereignty of this local universe. So his death upon the cross was never part of any plan connected with his mandate, other than that his death was needed to complete his life, the same way it has to be the end of other mortal lives here. But we will have a closer look at all this much later, when we get to the more exact story of his life on earth, many lessons after this one."

"The Daynals, Trinity Teacher Sons, engage in diverse educational ministry to local universes. Many of the heads of departments in the Melchizedek schools belong to this order, as do the staff members of countless universities; and large numbers are stationed on the morontia training worlds. They serve not only mortal ascenders; they are engaged in teaching services to seraphic beings and other natives of local creations. The Teacher Sons even now visit your world in preparation for the instauration of a spiritual age, one of cosmic enlightenment, which in the normal scheme of things would have occurred before now."

"Here ends this section, presented by a Perfector of Wisdom."

# Chapter 8

## Trinitized Sons of God

Lieu "Creator Sons are the makers and rulers of the local universes of time and space. Each one is different from every other, unique in nature as well as in personality; each is the 'only-begotten Son' of the deity ideal of his origin."

"These primary Paradise Sons are personalized as Michaels, starting as Creator Michaels, and when settled in supreme authority are Master Michaels."

"A Creator Son may choose the space site of his cosmic acitivity, after he studies similar efforts of his older brothers, and completes a long training period prior to that stage. As he develops his planning, he must consider:

1. Energy-matter; before any new transformations in this regard may be done a Creator Son must secure the consent and cooperation of the Infinite Spirit.
2. Creature designs and types; similarly, before any new style or type of creature is tried, the Son must arrange for the consent of the Eternal Son."

Lieu "It's time to examine the Trinity-Embraced Sons of God, a group of seven:

1. Mighty Messengers
2. Those High in Authority
3. Those without Name and Number

4. Trinitized Custodians
5. Trinitized Ambassadors
6. Celestial Guardians
7. High Son Assistants

"Mighty Messengers are an ascendant group of perfected mortals, who have passed through some test of loyalty, and are Trinity embraced after their acceptance into the Corps of the Finality."

"Those High in Authority are perfected mortals of superior administrative ability and experience. They are executives of the Ancients of Days."

"Those without Name and Number are outstanding ascendant leaders in spiritual comprehension and sometime serve as juror-judges."

"Trinitized Custodians are ascendant seraphim and translated midway creatures, who have attained the Corps of the Finality."

Lieu "Trinitized Ambassadors are recruited from the best minds of both Fatherfused and Sonfused ascendant personalities. They serve as emissaries of the Ancients of Days in emergency or reserve situations."

"The Celestial Guardians are Creature-trinitized sons. They are the officers of the courts of the Ancients of Days, and have never been spirit-spark infused."

"The High Son Assistants are a similar group, who function as personal aids to the governments of the Ancients of Days."

Erin "All this gets to be baffling, don't you think? How do you keep track?"

Lieu "As I've said before—I can jump in any place and run it off again. No credit to me, really, it's just on tap, ready to roll anytime. Now, I think it's time we had a look at the Solitary Messengers, okay?" Erin "You da boss."

"Solitary messengers are the first and senior order of high personalities created by the Infinite Spirit. At last report there were 7,690 trillion of them active in our superuniverse, and yes, they actually enjoy serving unaccompanied, all by themselves. But here, too, there is good reason—if they are too close to beings of their group, or entities which function similarly, their receptiveness to the circuits of intelligence is compromised, interfering with their effectiveness. One characteristic of their service and their status is that they have no organization or government unto themselves, or to report to—they are solitary messengers." These marvelous beings are active in seven groupings: they are Messengers of

1. the Paradise Trinity
2. the central universe circuit
3. the superuniverses
4. the local Universes
5. Undirected Assignment
6. Special Assignment
7. Revelators of Truth

"Note that these are not groupings of entities but of activities—they switch about among the latter as is deemed advisable. This order of messengers provide the only means by which the rulers of one super-universe can directly and effectively communicate with those of another."

"On special assignment these messengers routinely move at speeds of about half a million of our miles per our second of time, which comes close to an independence from time and space. Remember that their being persons adds much to the value of their services—they are true persons, yet endowed with nearly all of the attributes of impersonal spirit."

"Higher personalities of the Infinite Spirit obtain in seven divisions:

1. Solitary Messengers
2. Universe Circuit Supervisors
3. Census Directors
4. Personal Aids of the Infinite Spirit
5. Associate Inspectors
6. Assigned Sentinels
7. Graduate Guides

The first four of these have tremendous endowments of antigravity. Of the seven altogether, only the Messengers and the Personal aids roam the superuniverses—the other five each have some sort of home base or area of activity and responsibility."

"Census Directors are concerned with space time creatures only to the extent of those with intelligent will, each such emerging or dying is promptly recorded."

Lieu "The Universe Circuit Supervisors are dedicated to the special care of the spirit-energy circuits of all organized space, and are personalized enozoic."

"The Graduate Guides are devoted to the task of guiding the mortal graduates from the superuniverses through the Preheaven course of instruction and training in preparation for admission to Paradise and the Corps of the Finality. It is believed that Graduate Guides are evolved Preheaven Servitals."

"The Messenger Hosts of Space include the following orders of celestials:

1. Preheaven Servitals
2. Universal Conciliators
3. Technical Advisers
4. Custodians of Record on Paradise
5. Celestial Recorders
6. Morontia Companions
7. Paradise Companions.

"The Servitals, the 'midway creatures' of the Central Universe, are not to be regarded as being in menial servitude. Every fourth servital is more physical in type than the others, but they all serve on the educational worlds near the capitals of the superuniverses."

"Universal Conciliators also have every fourth one a semimaterial being. The other three form a referee trio, adjudicating administratively on matters of less than eternal import. All conciliators serve under the Acients of Days, and under the immediate direction of the Image Aids."

"The Technical Advisers are recruited from the following personality orders:

1. The Supernaphim
2. The Seconaphim
3. The Tertiaphim
4. The Omniaphim
5. The Seraphim
6. Certain Ascending Mortals
7. Certain Ascending Midwayers."

"On the eternal Isle, the Custodians of Records guard archives going back to

the personification of the Infinite Spirit."

"The Morontia Companions are friends to those ascenders who live the morontia life, acting more or less as gracious hosts, facilitating play and rest. They serve exclusively in the local universes."

"Members of the angelic hosts are appointed to serve as Paradise Companions, and these are not permanent assignments. They are often assisted in this by Paradise Citizens. In the case of your being accompanied on the Isle by the companion or close associate of your earthly career, then no permanent Paradise Companion will be assigned to you, but otherwise one will await your arrival. You will be warmly welcomed by temporary companions nonetheless."

"The pilgrims of time are transported past the dark gravity bodies surrounding the central universes by the transport personalities of the primary order of the seconaphim, operating from the headquarters of the seven superuniverses, to land on the receiving planet of Preheaven. At this point their deliverance from the uncertainties of time is complete, and the entry into a sonship cooperation with the Father fragment sets the stage for further development. There is a definite requirement to be met on each of the Preheaven circles; the course of these achievements is quantitative, qualitative, and experiential."

# Chapter 9

## Power by the Hour

Lieu "At the southern end of the vast Paradise domain, the masters of philosophy conduct elaborate courses in the seventy functional divisions of wisdom, seeking to coordinate the experiences and compose the knowledge of all who have access to their wisdom. Their methods by far surpass the word-memory approaches that prevail on earth."

"Here ends the section presented by a Perfector of Wisdom."

"Little has been imparted to earthlings about the controllers and regulators of the physical creation; we should spend some time on the Power Directors."

"They are living beings, in four groups:

1. Seven Supreme P Directors
2. Supreme Power Centers
3. Master Phys Controllers
4. Morontia Power Supervisors."

"The Supreme Power Directors are stationed on peripheral Paradise; they function singly when concerned with a superuniverse, but collectively when occupied with the Central Creation"

"The Supreme Power Centers function in these seven groups:

1. Supreme Center Supervisors
2. Preheaven Centers
3. Superuniverse Centers
4. Local Universe Centers
5. Constellation Centers
6. System Centers
7. Unclassified Centers."

"All of these are endowed with Third Source personality, great intelligence, and a high order of volitional capacity."

"One thousand Superuniverse Centers receive three currents of primary energy of ten segregations each at superuniverse headquarters, but seven specialized circuits of power issue forth therefrom, each of definite purpose."

"These power centers only guide material or semiphysical energy, and with physical gravity they only direct it by resisting its power."

"These are introductory remarks, going any further is not now advisable."

# Chapter 10

## Many Mansions

Lieu "The Master Force Organizers reside on Paradise but function all through the master universe, especially in unorganized space. They are neither creators nor creatures; they comprise two divisions:

1. Primary Eventuated
2. Associate Transcendental"

"Both work under the Architects of the Master Universe. The first group are nebulae creators. Until and unless the creation of a local universe is made known by the arrival of a Creator Son, the Associate Transcendentals will carry on from there until some change becomes appropriate."

"One thing I should mention about which we were given a caution: 'It is best that man not have an overrevelation; it stifles imagination'."

"The entire ascendant plan of mortal progression includes the practice of giving out to other beings new truth and experience as soon as acquired, in that way serving as teacher to those following close behind."

"All mortals of survival status in the custody of personal guardians of destiny personalize on the mansion worlds. Mortals who have not attained the tutelage of such guardians must rest in unconscious sleep until the judgment day of a new epoch, a new dispensation at the end of which a Son of God calls the rolls of the age and adjudicates the realm. It was said of Christ Michael that when he did ascend on high, 'He led a great multitude of captives'. These captives were the sleeping survivors from the days of Adam to the Master's resurrection."

"Ascending Father-fused mortals of time at the successful conclusion of their achievement of Paradise residence status enter the Corps of the Finality. Other members of this group are the following:

1. Preheaven Natives
2. Gravity Messengers
3. Adopted Seraphim
4. Glorified Material Sons
5. Glorified Midwayers"

"All six members take an oath of allegiance only to the Paradise Trinity."

Lieu "At this point it should be mentioned that the material recited thus far was sponsored, formulated, and put into English by a high commission of 24 administrators of the seventh superuniverse in accordance with a mandate issued by the Ancient of Days in the year A.D. 1934."

The Evolution of Local Universes

Lieu "The local universes of time and space are all evolutionary. The one in which your earth is located was launched by the creative plan of the God-man Jesus of Nazareth to whom we usually refer as Christ Michael."

"The preuniverse manipulation of space-force and the primordial energies are the work of the Paradise Master Force

Organizers, but when emergent energy becomes responsive to local or linear gravity, they retire in favor of the power directors of the surrounding superuniverse."

"When energy-matter has attained a certain stage in mass materialization the Creator Son and his companion Creative Spirit arrive, and work is begun on the construction of the architectural sphere which is to become the headquarter world of the projected local universe, while the planned development of the time space universe in the surrounding area is beginning to take its basic form."

Lieu "Presently, the physical layout of the universe completed, the Creator Son projects his plan of life creation, and forthwith the Creator Spirit comes into her fated status as a distinct personality and therewith springs into being the Bright and Morning Star, the chief executive of the local universe and personal associate of the Creator Son."

"The government of the local universe soon comes into being, from the supreme councils to the fathers of the constellations and the sovereigns of the local systems and in sequence, the Planetary Princes of the time space planets."

"From the headquarters of your local universe, it is more than 200,000 light years to the center of your superuniverse, buried in the Milky Way."

Erin "I have a question. When you are 'reciting' this material you seem to be speaking as if from some unknown entity's persona to me, the mortal recipient. Is that by design? Are you passing on the received words as the agent of the speaker to me, acting agent of the people for whom this material was indited?"

Lieu "Pretty much, yes. But you must remember that as far as we know, it comes to me already the result of what you might call an edited translation, and I have the sense that what I say too, is the result of an edited transmission—I say what I think will be most comprehensible and sensible to you, and/ or others. And this I do as best I can, while preserving the essentials of what I 'hear'."

Erin "So you hear all that and then give it to me as cleanly as you can."

Lieu "Tha's it, man, tha's it." Erin "Reverse poetry in redaction. So tell me, why aren't we using a tape recorder, to make a stable record of all this?"

Lieu "Isn't that obvious? We already have something better than that, the result of my training, which enables me to fish and choose for repetition whatever we might need to run through, for whatever reason."

Erin "What if something happens to you? One day you may fail to reappear."

Lieu "How many years has it been so far? Do you worry that tomorrow may not be another day? Have I ever failed to report for duty when I was needed?"

Erin "Not that I remember, but I have been anxious at times."

Lieu "Your anxiety, my Tarzan tainted philosophe, is not the measure of my constancy. Trust me, tomorrow's not coming to be is more likely than my failing to continue with you. And don't ask me how I know this, for I just do, so there."

Yet Erin cannot help but think 'And who the hell are you, my "friend", 'Just who the hell are you? And just what sort of "who" is <u>what</u> you are?'

Lieu "You should learn to relax, you know, none of this is ever going to hurt you in any way. This all is an opportunity such as never was and, chances are, never again will be—our understanding of the logistics of this whole chain of transactions is nowhere near as important as our responsibility to take it as it comes and do our best to give others as good as we got, in each and every sense. Your time will come, dear Erin lad, your time will come; on time."

Erin "Sounds good, I suppose. What else is there to do?"

Lieu "Some time back I mentioned the arrival of the Bright and Morning Star. He is Gabriel, a being like the Creator Son and the Creator Spirit, and partaking of their combined natures, sometimes he is spoken of as the brother of the Creator Son. But more specifically, he is the Son's personal administrative representative; during Michael's later bestowals, Gabriel was the actual director of universe affairs."

"Every local universe is blessed with the presence of some personalities from the Central Universe, and from Paradise. As representative from the Trinity to our Creator Son is Immanuel, at the head of this group of ambassadors. Immanuel is sometimes spoken of as the elder brother of Michael, and as such is often consulted by Gabriel when Michael is not available."

Lieu "When administrative ranks are more or less complete and settled, there is a new form of creative union between the C Son and the C Spirit. The personality offspring from this partnership is the original Melchizedek, the Father Melchizedek, who later collaborates with them to bring into existence the entire group of Melchizedeks. These beings concentrate not so much on administration as on practical procedures—but in Gabriel's absence it is the Father Melchizedek who functions as the chief executive of the local universe."

"The Melchizedeks approach sufficiently near to lower creature life to be able to work directly in the ministry of mortal uplift without necessarily incarnating."

"The Melchizedek who lived on earth at the time of Abram incarnated with permission of the Melchizedek receivers, who feared that spiritual truth was in jeopardy during that crisis of darkness. His mission was of good success."

"Near local universe headquarters the Melchizedeks have a world of their own, called Melchizedek, which is the pilot world of a circuit of seventy primary spheres, each of which is encircled by six tributary spheres, all of which group is often spoken of as the Melchizedek University."

Lieu "The Life Carriers. Life does not originate spontaneously; it is constructed according to plans formulated by Architects of Being, and appears on a planet either by direct importation or by the services of the Life Carriers of the local universe. "The Life Carriers are the offspring of: the Creator Son, the Universe Mother Spirit, and one of the three Ancients of Days. "In our local universe 100 million Life Carriers were created"

"Near the local universe headquarters there are seven primary spheres of Life Carriers, each with six satellites, and the seven are arranged as follows:

1. The Life Carrier headquarters
2. The life planning sphere
3. The life conservation sphere
4. The sphere of life evolution
5. The sphere of life associated with mind
6. The sphere of mind and spirit
7. The sphere of unrevealed life.

On the headquarter world are situated the seven central emplacements of the adjutant mind-spirits. The fact that the construction plans and arrangements of life are based on the number seven is a strong indication that life belongs not in the physical but in the spiritual realm; in contrast, physical reality is based on the number ten—the decimal system."

Lieu "There are over one million fundamental or cosmic chemical formulas which are parental to the formulations of the life plasm under consideration at any time, and earth being what is called a decimal planet, or one on which an experimental approach is approved for a special attempt to implement a new or improved life pattern or formulation, the preparations which were worked out for this planet were more exhaustive, more varied, and purposefully speculative, than is usually the case."

"The corps of Life Carriers commissioned to plant life on a new world usually consists of 100 senior carriers, 100 assistants, and 1,000 custodians. They do not always bring life; sometimes, as in the case of earth, they bring formulas and instructions which they use to build life plasm from the materials gathered, and impart to that the spark needed to activate it into living substance. Note that they only convey the spark—it actually comes from the Creation Spirit of the local universe. The Life Carriers are, however, living catalytic ambiences/supports."

"The Life Carriers are normally allowed about half a million of the planet's years to foster the development of the life they have initiated and they are permitted to manipulate the environment to some degree towards that end, but when they have succeeded in producing a being with will, with moral decision making, and spiritual choice, their work is done and they depart."

The Seven Adjutant Mind-Spirits "These life-mind emplacements always accompany the Life Carriers to a new planet. They are not entities, nor are they persons—they are better described as circuits. They are ministers to the lower levels of experiential mind, as follows:

1. The spirit of intuition
2. The spirit of understanding
3. The spirit of courage
4. The spirit of knowledge
5. The spirit of counsel
6. The spirit of worship
7. The spirit of wisdom."

"The first five of these function in the animal kingdom, but are essential in the human being for all seven to develop, towards the end that soul and morontia dimensions of a being with spiritual aspirations be propitiously enfounded. Mind is a divinity bestowal, but not immortal without spirit-personal insight."

Caveat . . . "Life is both mechanistic and vitalistic; it is something different from all energy manifestations—even the life of the simply physical creatures is not inherent in matter. Life springs only from life! Mind springs only from mind! Spirit springs only from a spirit ancestry!"

"When the life formulas and the vital patterns are ready, the Life Carrier can provide the spark to start life, but the resulting living organism is devoid of two proclivities: there is no mind; there is no reproductive capacity. For mind, the assistance of the Adjutant Mind Spirits is required; for reproduction, a specific intervention of the Universe Mother Spirit is necessary."

Lieu "This concludes lesson 9, which was indited by a Vorondadek Son stationed on earth as an observer; by request of the Melchizedek Chief of the Supervising Revelatory Corps."

Lieu "Universe Aids include the following seven orders:

1. Bright and Morning Stars
2. Brilliant Evening Stars
3. Archangels
4. Most High Assistants
5. High Commissioners

6. Celestial Overseers
7. Mansion World Teachers."

"In the first group there is only one, whom we have met . . . Gabriel, and he did function by himself for quite a while, until he was provided with a personal staff of Brilliant Evening Stars. Many of those started as seraphim."

"Archangels classify personality records and identification sureties, file them, and preserve them, during the time between mortal death and repersonalization."

"Most High Assistants are from outside the local universe, come to help as they are needed, in the most various assignments, and they are of the most diverse orders of Sons. They always number in the millions."

"High Commissioners are Spirit-fused ascendant mortals, not destined to attain Paradise; they do eventually become enrolled in the Corps of Perfection. They begin their services as race commissioners, spokespersons on behalf of disadvantaged mortal races; friends of the courts in many situations, speaking for those who are not in attendance to speak for themselves."

"Celestial Overseers are a recruited corps serving in connection with the education of mortal ascenders, who themselves may sometime serve thus."

"The Mansion World Teachers are recruited and glorified cherubim, about whom we shall learn more later in these readings."

Lieu 'The Material Sons of God.' "When a creative liaison between the Creator Son and the Universe Mother Spirit has completed its cycle, then does the Creator Son personalize in dual form his last concept of being, thus finally confirming his own and original dual origin—in and of himself he then creates the beautiful and superb Sons and Daughters of the material order of universe sonship. This is the origin of the original Adam and Eve of each system of the local universe. They are a reproducing order of sonship, male and female."

"On a planetary mission the Material Son and Daughter are charged to found the Adamic race, designed to amalgamate with the inhabitants so as to upgrade the planetary mortal races. It often happens that an uncertainty arises as to the exact nature of instances of mixed ancestry, giving rise to creatures whose nature falls somewhere between the evolutionary races and the Material Sons, and they are thus called midwayers, being partly spiritual and partly material-evolutionary. Their longevity borders on the eternal, from the mortal ascenders' point of view. However, we will talk more about them later."

Lieu 'The Origin of Seraphim.' "Seraphim are created by the Universe Mother Spirit, 41,472 at a time, dating from the time of her personalizing. Angels do not have material bodies—they can see us, but we cannot normally see them. We commonly refer to them as daughters of the Spirit, though they are asexual; they neither marry nor are given in marriage."

Lieu "Angels do not sit in judgment on mortals; neither should we do so."

Erin "And are you mortal? Am I permitted to judge you? What would I need?"

Lieu "That's an interesting thought. In the dictum I just recited we are enjoined to not judge other mortals, and I think the implication is that we have no such authority because we are on a par with them, but more than that: from the fact that angels do not judge us or our peers we should take the lesson that it requires something more than just being superior in some way(s) to those facing judgment—and it strikes me we have already come across the answer to what that something might be. Do you remember our coming up with it?"

Erin "No, I don't recall anything in that vein. Have I forgotten, and not you?"

Lieu "I'm not sure whether I made it clear at the time, so let me try again. The executive part of a trial at law must never be the prerogative of an individual, nor of any entity representing only an individual. If a judicial pronouncement, or a judgment, be made or enacted, it should be either by a committee that has been selected to speak for the plurality of those with an interest in the matter at issue, or else by an entity with such tried and tested experience as has enabled him to earn the unquestioning confidence of all parties composing that plurality."

Erin "It sounds familiar, and I sure can't come up with a better idea than that!"

Lieu "Amen." Erin "Amen?" Lieu "Yes, let it be so."

Erin "Now just hold on a minute. I asked if you are mortal, remember? And I've asked you that before, so how about an answer? Are . . . . You . . . . Mortal?"

Lieu "Very good, Erin. Very good indeed—it is a valid question."

Erin "And so, it deserves an honest answer, yes? Get off the fence already!"

Lieu "I'm very sorry, Erin, I cannot do that now. I well knew that you would be at me again about this, but I have my instructions; I have been advised that it's premature to give you a full answer, even if I knew it myself, which I do not. When we get further into all this there will be a better time. They will let me know more than I do now, and then I'll be able to tell you what you need to know about it."

Erin "Okay. But it's hard to imagine that you do not know what you really are."

Lieu "I'm quite sure it's harder for me than for you." Erin "Right—sorry!"

Erin has finished the upgrading of the house, and, with an eye on logging off the timber on the property, he has bought two big steel wheel John Deere tractors. The less old one has a good power take-off on it, so he has installed a liftable blade on the front so he can snow plow the long driveway in winter. The other one he has set up to belt power a little sawmill he got at an auction, so now he can make his own lumber as well. He quite enjoys rumbling around with the two primitive monsters, even the startup of the two horizontal seven inch piston engine with the heavy 18 inch manual flywheel. And strange to relate, there is an extra little pup tank that takes water, and he can regulate how much of it to release with the gas after the engine is nicely warmed up. In a way quite amazing, that he can burn water in this very simple engine setup. But then, water consists of hydrogen and oxygen, right?

Lieu "In all essential endowments, cherubim and sanobim are similar to seraphim; they serve in pairs, each a positive or a negative expression. They normally assist the seraphim, but only in the local universe, and not attending human beings directly. They are most efficient in the borderland work of the physical, morontial, and spiritual domains, depending on their achievement status. Here again, every fourth one is quasi-material, and are to the morontia spheres about what the midway creatures are to the evolutionary planets."

The Midway Creatures "These unique creatures appear on the majority of inhabited worlds, and always on decimal planets such as earth. They are of two types, primary and secondary. The Primary Midwayers are the more spiritual, derived from the modified ascendant-mortal staffs of the Planetary Princes, and always number 50,000. Secondary Midwayers derive from the planetary biologic uplifters, the Adams and Eves, or from their progeny; they average 50,000."

"Neither of these groups is an accident; both are part of the plans of the universe architects and the Life Carriers. Primary Midwayers resemble angels more than mortals; the secondary are more like humans. Sooner or later the earth-accredited midwayers will enter the ranks of ascending Sons of God and progress towards the Isle of Paradise in company with the very earth brethren whom they served so effectively while on the planet."

The Number Seven "There is in all matter, notwithstanding the decimal constitution of energy, a reminder of the underlying seven-creating reality, in the sevenfold electronic organization of prematter. The atomic world displays a periodic characterization recurring in sevens, manifesting throughout the periodic table of elements, more bold in the lighter elements at the beginning, and tapering off to the heavier. Properties and characteristics repeat by sevens—remarkable! As well, the sevenfold color grouping in the spectrum: red, orange, yellow, green, blue, indigo, and violet presents another phenomenon in this vein."

"While in practical applications the laws of nature seem to operate in the dual realms of the physical and the spiritual, in reality they are one. The universe of universes in toto is mind planned, mind made, and mind administered. Note, however, the mind in this statement is neither material nor creature mind; it is spirit-mind, functioning on and from creator levels of divine reality. Thus, to find the truth value in this claim about total mind, time-space minds would have to exercise a reach beyond their natural proclivities, a leap of faith is needed, a degree of spirit identification. Remember that the spirit is the creative reality; the physical counterpart is the time-space reflection, the foggy shadow, thereof."

Lieu 'Speaking now in the voice of the Archangel reciting': "I cannot, with exclusive spirit vision, perceive the building in which this narrative is being translated and recorded. A Divine Counselor who chances to be here sees it even less. We are helped in approximating how these material structures appear to you, by viewing a spirit counterpart projected by one of our attending energy transformers. The higher forms of spirits freely pass through ordinary matter."

Lieu: 'The Thought Recorders' "These artisans form seven groups:

1. Thought Preservers
2. Concept Recorders
3. Ideograph Recorders
4. Promoters of Oratory
5. Broadcast Directors
6. Rhythm Recorders
7. Morontia Recorders

They care for the preservation of the noblest thoughts that come into their purview, in the standard language that is most suitable for the specific applications and goals prevailing in their domain."

"Each local universe has its own standard language, as does each super-universe, and the higher orders of beings are presumed to be proficient in both, but when the need arises, translators are readily accessible and cooperative."

"Concept Recorders deal in concept pictures and idea patterns, the essentials of which are difficult for the time-space mind to comprehend or imagine."

"Ideograph Recorders engage in even greater degrees of abstraction and more refined techniques of compact representation, as one might expect."

"Broadcast Directors are involved in editing, translating, collating, and most efficiently preparing broadcasts in a plethora of applications and transmissions."

"Morontia Recorders, roughly speaking, are group photographers active in the morontia realms of existence. You will see."

Lieu 'The System Government' "The System Sovereign is normally supported by two or three Lanonandek Sons, but currently there are seven, due to the difficulties stemming from the Lucifer rebellion. They are assisted by the twelve members of the superuniverse executive council."

Lieu 'The Twenty-Four Counselors' "John the Revelator called these the four and twenty elders. Some were chosen from the eight races of humans on earth. Some others are: Onagar, mastermind from pre Planetary Prince time; Mansant, great teacher post Planetary Prince; Adam, discredited but rehabilitated Material Son of Eden; Enoch, first on earth to fuse with Father-spark while alive; Moses the emancipator; Elijah, a translated soul of spiritual brilliance; Machiventa Melchizedek, enfleshed as mortal at time of Abram, and declared vice-gerent Planetary Prince of earth; John the Baptist; 1-2-3 the First, leader of the loyal midwayers. Some seats are temporarily vacant, others held in reserve.

"They have been Christ Michael's personal agents since his attainment of full sovereignty, and are also the designated agents in service to Gabriel."

Lieu 'The Material Sons' "At the last millennial registration there were 161.4 million material sons and daughters of citizenship status on local system capitals. They enjoy an advanced self governing civilization, and are of great help to ascenders as companions and as a resource of counseling expertise."

Lieu 'The Melchizedek Schools' "On the seven mansion worlds, the detention planets, unfused mortals are in training to develop themselves towards the spiritualizing which they failed to ensoul before death, and this is done under the tutelage of the Melchizedeks in their training schools."

Lieu '<u>The Mansion Worlds</u>'

"There are fifty-six spheres encircling the Local System headquarter world, and around the first of these are seven satellites known as The Mansion Worlds."

"When a system is settled in light and life, and the mansion worlds one by one cease to serve as mortal training stations, they serve as residence to Finaliters."

Lieu '<u>The Resurrection of the Dead—reassembly of Creature Personality</u>' "The mortal mind transcripts and such memory patterns as have proved enozoice as having some spiritual import, are reclaimed from the Father fragment; the creature mind-matrix and the potentials of identity are likewise relinquished by the seraphic destiny guardian. The spirit-mind trust of the Father spark, and the morontia-soul trust of the guardian are reunited/resurrected in the still mortal ascender. Thus the real and conscious reassembly of actual and complete personality takes place in the resurrection halls of mansonia number one."

Lieu '<u>The First Mansion World</u>.' "On the first mansion world, or one of higher number in cases of advanced status, all survivors must pass the requirements of the parental commission from their native planet. The present earth commission consists of twelve parental couples who have experienced rearing at least three children to the age of puberty. No ascending mortal can escape the experience of rearing children, and fathers must pass this testing as well as mothers—every child needs a father and a mother."

"There are probationary nurseries to accommodate infants who have died before achieving identity status—when they reach the age of moral choice they are given the same opportunities as any other ascender candidate, to continue in the normal path."

"On each of the mansion worlds ascenders will have clearance to visit any earlier worlds, and to socialize with mortal ascenders at different states of progress."

# Chapter 11

## The Lucifer Rebellion

Lieu: 'The Second Mansion World' "A newly developed and suitably adjusted morontia body is acquired at each advance to the next mansion world; you sleep during the seraphic transport and awake with your new body in the resurrection halls, with personality intact."

"In the morontia body you eat, drink, and rest, but food and drink are totally utilized—there is no waste. On the Second Mansion World intellectual conflict and mental disharmony are resolved more fully, to the extent usually comparable with the post Magisterial Son culture on ideal evolutionary spheres."

"On the first two mansion worlds training was mostly focused on remedies for various shortcomings—on the Third Mansion World begins in earnest the overall advancement in the building of greater insights into philosophical and more metaphysical issues."

"The Fourth Mansion World is where ascenders become more conscious of God-knowing, God-revealing, God-seeking, and God-finding."

"On the Fifth Mansion World there is a focus on learning the language of the local universe, and that of the superuniverse. With the attendant expansion of overarching concepts and symbology, this results in a real birth of cosmic consciousness at this stage." "The Sixth Mansion World is where an understanding of the various layers of universe administration and governance is gradually built. The final completion of the fusion with the Father fragment is often another achievement at this time. The signal recognition of this success is a ceremony in which this pronouncement is made: 'This is a beloved son in whom I am well pleased'." "The Seventh Mansion World is the graduation locale, where there is the official eradication of any last remnants of any unspiritual planetary vestiges—the departure to the superuniverse headquarters will be as a citizen of a new level of the greater cosmos."

Erin "No small matter, then. Hard to imagine all that. It's like building seven careers, and each of them starting at kindergarten and going through postgraduate work before going on to the next layer of qualifying existence."

Lieu "Boggles one's little mind, doesn't it? John the Revelator saw a vision of the arrival of a class of advancing mortals from the seventh mansion world to their first heaven, called Jerusem. He recorded: 'And I saw as it were a sea of glass mingled with fire; and those who had gained the victory over the beast that was originally in them and over the image that persisted through the mansion worlds and finally over the last mark and trace, standing on the sea of glass, having the harps of God, and singing the song of deliverance from mortal fear and death.' ("The harps of God refer to a morontia contrivance which enables the immature morontia sensory mechanism to receive space communication.")

"Paul also had a view of the ascendant-citizen corps of perfecting mortals on Jerusem, for he wrote: 'But you have come to Mount Zion and to the city of the living God, the heavenly Jerusalem, and to an innumerable company of angels, to the grand assembly of Michael, and the spirits of just men being made perfect'."

Lieu "Erin, has it struck you that we've just been getting a bit of a rerun of the life and mission of Jesus in that last section?" Erin "No, not particularly, how?"

Lieu "Well, first there was that bit about 'my beloved son, in whom I am well pleased' right?" Erin "Yes, I noticed that, but then we went on with much more."

Lieu "Right, there were quotations from St John and St Paul, all indited in New Testament times, and therefore, all about Jesus. Remember, Jesus was fully man AND fully God, so he had to go through essentially the same sequence of events, had to experience the same stages of progression as other mortal ascenders, that being the path that has to be traversed as part of dying and achieving heaven, which would have been, one must suppose, quite smooth sailing for him." Erin "Of course, it's all quite clear. It's just never been laid out like that to me." Lieu "Worth remembering, me lad, worth remembering."

Lieu "Back to the topic of the day. Only the seven worlds surrounding the finaliters' sphere of the local system are called mansion worlds, but all 56 of the system transition abodes, as well as the higher spheres around the constellations and the universe headquarters, are called morontia worlds. All of these worlds are architectural, or made-to-order worlds, comprised of a different configuration of elements, and a unique energy organization called 'morontia material'."

"In the morontia life the spirit will become a real part of your personality, and as you successively pass through some 570 progressive transformations, you ascend from the material to the more spiritual estate of creature life."

"Paul learned of the morontia worlds and morontia material—he wrote: 'They have in heaven a better and more enduring substance, as in the city which has foundations, whose builder and maker is God'."

"As morontia progressors you will remain in full contact with the material world and personalities, although you will increasingly discern and fraternize with spiritual beings. Morontia Companions will be of help to a great extent. Midway creatures are your closest of kin, then the morontia cherubins, and the Morontia Companions have the furthest to reach across the divide that separates."

Lieu 'Inhabited Worlds' "The system to which our planet belongs does not have the usual complement of one thousand evolutionary worlds, as it is still in process of development—at present it contains 619 inhabited planets; our earth has the serial number of 606 in this system. There are thirty-six worlds approaching the life endowment stage, several of which are now being made ready for Life Carriers. Evolution is the rule of human development, but the process differs significantly on various worlds. Life is sometimes initiated in one location, at other times it might occur in three, as it did on earth. On the atmospheric worlds life usually has a marine origin, as on earth, but it is not always the case. The vegetable form of life always precedes the animal, and the transition is not capricious—it follows a smooth developmental sequence, each favorable strain giving rise to a consequential new animal form."

Lieu 'Planetary Physical Types' "There are seven (as one might expect) distinct physical types of life forms, each suited for a specific sort of planet:

1. The Atmospheric type
2. The Elemental type
3. The Gravity type
4. The Temperature type
5. The Electric type
6. The Energizing type
7. The Unnamed types"

"The atmospheric types are typically instantiated by the inhabitants of our earth. There are three sub-categories, those who can tolerate almost no air, the nonbreathers; those of little air, the sub-breathers; and those of air in less than optimum states, the super-breathers."

"The elemental types are creatures who cope with extreme conditions, as when a planet is far from being ready to provide the necessary elements in anything approaching a stable and negotiable panoply of life supports."

"The gravity types contend with planets of less than ideal size and density; some of the larger planets' inhabitants are around thirty inches in height; and some of the very small are occupied by those of ten feet or more."

"The temperature types are those who cope with greater heat or greater cold than the average. The earth, except for atypical times such as droughts or ice ages, is in this respect of a fairly even range of warmth."

"The electric types contend with extreme conditions of electric, magnetic, or even electronic/chemical situations. There are ten sub types in this category."

"The energizing types are specialized in dealing with less than optimum arrays of nutrition and energy, and they constitute six variants, of which there is one that is specifically limited to the midway creatures."

"The unnamed types have various coping strategies to do with anatomical modification, physiological adaptation, and electrochemical adjustments, none of which affect the intellectual or spiritual potentials."

Lieu 'Evolutionary Will Creatures' "All mortals of will dignity are erect animals, bipeds. Mortals all have the same struggles with microscopic foes in their early days, though not so extensively as on earth. The length of life varies from twenty-five years on primitive worlds to nearly five hundred on older spheres. With the arrival of the first Father fragment on a space time world, guardian seraphim also make their appearance—throughout the life-lapse period of sleeping survivors the spiritual values of the immortal souls are held as a sacred trust by the personal or the group guardian seraphim, to be returned to the ascender upon repersonalization on a mansion world, where the Father spark will also rejoin the ascendant candidate."

Lieu 'The Planetary Princes' "The entire staff of a world ruler consists of personalities of the Infinite Spirit and certain types of higher evolved beings and ascending mortals from other worlds. Such a staff averages about 1,000 and as the planet progresses, may be increased to 100,000 or more, simply by request to the System Sovereign. All Planetary Princes are under the jurisdiction of Gabriel. On occasion seraphic helpers and Melchizedeks are visible to planet mortals."

Lieu 'The Prince's Corporeal Staff' "The prince usually takes with him a group of volunteer ascenders from the local system headquarters—they are non-fused morontia progressors who temporarily revert to a former material state. At the time of the next adjudication, these staff members are usually removed from the planet, assigning their duties to their offspring and to deserving native volunteers. They seldom mate with the world races, but do mate among themselves. Two classes of beings result from this mating: primary midwayers, and successors to the staff members."

"The work of training and educating the mortals of the planet, in physical as well as more enlightening domains, was progressing nicely when, about 200,000 years ago, the Lucifer rebellion had such impact on the Prince that he renounced his calling, and made it his mission to assist Lucifer's henchmen in any way he could. The schools and the teachings which had become so promising, fell into disarray, and were of no further effect."

Lieu 'The Planetary Adams' "The material or sex Sons and Daughters are the offspring of the Creator Son—in this the Creator Spirit does not participate; they are specific to the life pattern of the local system. Material Sons vary in height from eight to ten feet, and they glow with a radiant violet hue. They enjoy a dual nutrition—their immortal existence is maintained by the direct intake of sustaining cosmic energies. Should they fail in their mission, or consciously rebel, they are isolated, cut off from their source of light and life, so that material death will be the long term consequence."

"The progeny of Material Sons have decreasing immortality with succeeding generations. The original parents can be seen by the planetary mortals, who can also learn to speak with them, and even procreate with them although that is not permissible. If all goes well on the planet, Adams and Eves can live indefinitely."

"Adams and Eves are semimaterial creatures and thus not capable of normal seraphim transport—they must first undergo dematerialization, which takes about three standard days, and the reversal thereof is accomplished with the participation of a Life Carrier, and it takes from ten to twenty-eight earth days."

"On earth, due to the devious machinations of the Prince, who had been misled by the Lucifer rebellion, all did not go well, so that even if Adam and Eve did not get involved in the rebellion, they did give in to the blandishments of the planetary prince, and ended up straying into a miscarriage of their mission."

"The fifth order of angels, planetary helpers, are attached to the program of the material sons, usually numbering 100,000. It was the leader of this group who remonstrated with the pair in the garden about their conduct."

"Descendants of the material sons are of two groups, the physical children and the secondary midwayers, ordinarily invisible planetary ministers who often contribute greatly to the advancement of planetary civilization, and participate in the policing of insubordinate minorities." 'Here ends the section presented by a Lanonandek Son'

Lieu 'The Lucifer Rebellion' "Lucifer was a brilliant primary Lanonandek Son, who had experienced service in many systems, had been a high counselor of his group, and was distinguished for wisdom, sagacity, and efficiency. When commissioned by the Melchizedeks, he was designated one of the hundred most able and brilliant of more than 700,000 of his kind."

Lieu "Lucifer was the chief executive of a great system of 607 inhabited worlds, but 200,000 years ago, earth time, he issued a manifesto proclaiming himself the ruler above God, of the local system, disallowing all other super-vision. He denounced the location of legislative activities on constellation headquarters and the conduct of judicial affairs on the universe capital. The entire administrative cabinet of Lucifer were sworn in publicly as a body, to be the officers of the new administrative government of the 'liberated worlds and systems'. He defied all his superiors, who took little note of his doings."

"Lucifer was permitted fully to establish and thoroughly to organize his rebel government before Gabriel made any effort to contest the right of secession, but the Constellation Fathers did immediately confine these activities to the local system of Satania. Since Michael had not at this time established his personal sovereignty over the local universe, the Creator Son decided, in conference with Immanuel, that Lucifer would be allowed to work out his destiny with no check or hindrance. Gabriel, however, elected to assume command of the loyal hosts of Satania, and held up for totem the banner of Michael, consisting of three azure blue concentric rings on a white background."

"The Lucifer rebellion was system wide—thirty-seven planetary princes swung their administrations to the side of the archrebel; 647,156 Material Sons in Satania were lost, and large numbers of midwayers as well."

# Chapter 12

## The Dawn of Willful Man

Lieu "Not much was heard of Lucifer on earth, since he assigned his first lieutenant Satan to advocate his cause on earth—thus in ancient times it was Satan who was known as the arch rebel, and the fallen Prince of earth as the devil. Since the creatures who resisted all the efforts of the perfidious rebels to lead them astray needed guidance and governance, in just over two years of system time a replacement administration was instituted in Satania, led by the new system sovereign, Lanaforge. "Michael was not yet fully sovereign over the local universe, so although the Ancients of Days sustained the Constellation Fathers in their seizure of the system government, no decisions were enacted regarding the many appeals concerning the fate of Lucifer and Satan associates."

"Notwithstanding that being the case, no fallen spirit ever did have the power to invade the minds or harass the souls of ascendant mortals—where there is supposedly an instance of possession by devils or demons, in actual fact it is a matter of an evolutionary creature of imperfect will, giving way to his private failings, his own debased tendencies, his own assent to impending sin. Neither Satan nor Caligastia has had any power to encroach on the free will of an ascendant mortal since Jesus suffered his earthly cross."

Erin "Wow! I bet there's millions of people who either do not know, or simply do not understand, what you just said."

Lieu "I'm afraid so, Erin—I'm afraid so. So hang onto that, hang onto it tight." Erin "But tell me again, are you totally sure of that? Are you still secure in the truth of all these things you've been spieling over me all this time, for so long?"

Lieu "I'm not really comfortable with that term 'spieling,' guv. Too close to the German word 'spiel' which I believe means play, or to play. Reminds me of the title *Homo Ludens*, or 'man playing'. In no sense of any of these are we playing."

Erin "Okay, let me snug it up a bit. Are the things you have been telling me in these last years infallible? Should I have been ascribing to them a scriptural type of authenticity?" Lieu "Oh my. We went over all that, don't you remember?"

Erin "Obviously not well enough. Could we have another go?"

Lieu "Alright, we agreed that might be good to do from time to time, but not today, not tonight—you need to get some rest, and I'd like to line up my ducks."

Erin "Goodnight my little Lieu, goodnight."

A lot of things have changed for Erin and Freya—four boys and a girl are in the picture. Erin has been in the life insurance business for some time, and has been buying properties; they now have a dozen mobile homes, eight private dwellings, two muliplexes, a partnership in a service station, and another in a TV and appliances facility. This last year has been especially busy, what with his doing his own maintenance on all that property, and doing the bookkeeping for the partnerships and his own activities.

He has been going to college in Chemlupe, taking accounting, and in conjunction with that an evening course in income tax. He thought he might fail that one, since he early stopped going to classes, for being too busy. Strange though, after not even writing the final, he got an A anyway—a wonder!

Lieu "Hello Erin. How did you make out with your income tax?"

Erin "You mean the course? I did alright with that—thought you would know."

Lieu "No, I meant the filing of your return. You did file? On time?"

Erin "Yes and no. I was just about ready to work on it when I realized I just did not have the time, so I got someone to do it for me. And you know what bloody happened? I have to pay income tax! That's the very first time, too. Ironic."

Lieu "Hmmnn—makes me wonder how accurately and correctly you did your financials and your filing in the previous years. How's your conscience doing?"

Erin "My conscience is just fine, thank you. I had to answer some questions on occasion, but there was no problem, no problem at all. All is well that ends."

Lieu "That ends well, yes. Sometimes an ending is not clear for a while."

"But, we must do what we are here to do, and that is: infallibility. That question is surprisingly simple, as it boils down to one simple caveat: No revelation that has been received, translated, transcribed, or conveyed in any manner involving the mind or hand of any mortal, can be rigorously adjudged infallible. Infallibility can be ascribed to God, and God alone. Mind you, as we learn more about the reach and limit of the referent in that statement, we will find that infallibility can obtain in somewhat wider scope than is implied thereby. However, no need to be too much a purist in this sort of thing, since we always have a touchstone in the Father spark within us to sound it out for tonal verity."

Erin "So now who's talking philosophy? Metaphysics no less."

Liue "Do you forget our minds are sort of linked by now? I can tell, you understand me very well, so do not bluster, do not cavil, do not protest in vacuo."

Erin "Yes dear, tonight you have a headache. I do understand."


Lieu "Michael, upon attaining his supreme sovereignty, petitioned the Ancients of Days for authority to intern all personalities involved in the Lucifer rebellion. This petition was granted with one exception: Satan was allowed to visit apostate princes until another Son of God should be accepted by their worlds, or the adjudication of the case of Gabriel vs Lucifer should commence."

"Satan did make such visits, right up to the time of these revelations, when the first hearing of that trial was launched. Since then temporary planetary regimes have been established on the isolated worlds, and Satan has himself been interned on the Jerusem prison worlds. We believe that all rebels who will ever accept mercy have done so."

Lieu 'Translation of Living Mortals' "It happens, on occasion, that a space time mortal has made enough progress in spiritualization and soul development that the time is right for fusion with the Father fragment. Should this occur on a presettled world such as earth (remember Enoch and Elijah) the candidate may be lifted off the ground, so the ensuing body-destroying fire will not do damage to others nearby. The ascender, then, will bypass the mansion worlds, and proceed directly to the morontia existence."

Lieu "Usually an evolutionary world will not advance to settledness in light and life until it hosts one blended race, one consensually developed language, one final and consensual religion, and one final and consensual philosophy."

Lieu 'The History of Earth' "We must backtrack a bit, and spend some time reviewing more closely the origin, the manner of its making, and the story of the development, of the planet earth—so herewith begins our lesson 13."

Lieu "Your planet earth is of origin in your sun, which in turn originated in the Andronover nebula, when it was part of your local universe."

"987 billion years ago acting inspector 811,307 of the seventh superuniverse reported to the Ancient of Days that space conditions favored the initiation of materialization in an easterly segment of the superuniverse."

"900 billion years back a permit was recorded authorizing the dispatch of a force organizer and staff to the location in question, to begin that materialization. 875 billion years ago the enormous Andronover nebula, number 876,926 was duly initiated; conditions were suitable for power directors and physical controllers."

Erin "Now wait just a minute here. If memory serves correctly, our earthly astronomers peg the age of this planet at around sixteen to eighteen billions of our years. What about that? Sounds like one hell of a discrepancy to me."

Lieu "For sure, and that's exactly what makes the explanation so eminently credible. I think we discussed the cyclical nature of the mechanism by which the organized and occupied sections of space are supplied with the power and the energy to keep them functioning and in homeostatic suspension for ages on end, Have you forgotten, or is it coming back to you?" Erin "It sounds familiar, yes."

Leiu "Right. The cosmos is 'fed' by Paradise. Pervaded, or charged space flows outward from nether Paradise to wash over/throughout all of organized space, and that motion is what looks to our astronomers like an expanding universe. What they have not had opportunity to observe, is that after a billion years of the outward breath, there is another billion years of the unpervaded or discharged space coming back to nether Paradise, constituting the 'inward' breath, and that 'exhalant' fills one cone-out area above Paradise, and another cone-out below it. Upon completion, the cycle starts all over again. Recharged space hurtles out, and the universe expands again; a two billion year cycle."

"Our astronomers, having convinced themselves that they are watching a depleting Big Bang, have done the calculation in regression of that expansion to arrive at what they conceive to be the big bang initiating Moment/Singularity, which they agree to have occurred some seventeen billion years ago. So you see, it's more or less a question of optics—wherein lies the confusion; the seeing eye being tied in to the wiring through the brain that ratio ad quem is affected."

Erin "Now I'm getting the impression that you're playing with the language a bit more than necessary, Minerva— Paradise imparting the breath of life to the cosmos, then taking it back and giving it another shot, and so on and so on in two billion year gasps of rescuscitation!"

Lieu "Alright now, enough of the poetry—let's carry on with creating earth."

"All evolutionary material creations are born of circular gaseous nebulae, which usually become spiral as they develop and give birth to suns, and when that process has run its course, they settle into clusters of stars with satellites."

"800 billion years ago Andronover was well established, and materialization was taking place as planned. 700 billion years back physical controllers were dispatched to nine surrounding centers to help maintain stability as the primary nebula reached maximum size and began increasing its rate of rotation."

"600 billion years ago maximum mass was achieved, and the gas cloud held shape as a flattened spheroid, and was starting to become spiral. The stage was set for converting space gases into organized matter. Two spiral arms emerged, and the central volume contracted somewhat as gravity took its toll."

"500 billion years back the first Andronover sun was born, and 400 billion years ago the enozoic period began, with smaller suns returning to the core. About a million years later Michael selected this area for his universe building, and during the following million years the architectural groups of planets were begun. Local system headquarters have been under construction until about one billion years ago. 300 billion years ago solar circuits were well established, and the local universe was recognized and placed on record."

"200 billion years back the outer regions had stabilized and life implantation was underway. 100 billion years ago heat was gaining on gravity, and the secondary career of a nebula saw a spectacular period of sun dispersion."

"Six billion years back was the terminal breakup, which also marked the birth of our sun, number 1,013,572 which was 56th from the last. Five billion years ago our sun had achieved relative stability, but 4.5 billion years back the enormous Angona system was approaching, and soon there were gaseous emissions being pulled away from our sun, the roots of which at times fell back, while the tips began their development into solar meteorites."

"500,000 years later the closest approach of Angona saw a disruption of our sun, with two columns of gases emerging from opposite sides, one of them being drawn away by Angona, the other developing into the twelve planets of our solar system. Had the planets been drawn off by solar rotation, they would travel in the plane of that rotation, but as it is, they adopted one shaped by the plane of the extrusion, with the exception of a retrograde motion occasioned by the near approach of three Angona tributaries."

"2.5 billion years ago the earth was about one tenth its present mass, and was growing steadily by meteoric accretion. 1.5 billion years back earth was two thirds its present size, and the moon had stabilized as it now is, though it kept losing atmosphere to the earth. It was an era of tremendous volcanic activity."

"900 million years ago a commission determined that our planet would be suitable as a decimal planet—a life experiment station, and Life Carriers were notified that new patterns of mechanical, chemical, and electrical mobilization would be applicable."

Lieu "Ancient preocean rocks in northeastern Canada, around Hudson Bay have been heated, bent, twisted, upcrumpled, and all in the absence of any life."

"Throughout the oceanic ages enormous layers of fossil-free stratified stone were deposited, and this by chemical precipitation—any fossils to be found there later were the result of chance admixture. During this period the earth crust was very unstable, but there was as yet no mountain building. Land mass increased until about ten percent of the planet surface rose above the waters."

"850 million years back the first stabilization of the crust began, most of the metals having settled towards the center of the globe. Volcanic eruptions and earthquakes became less frequent, and the atmosphere cleared of noxious gases. 800 million years ago saw increased continental emergence, with the areas of America, Europe, Africa, Australia, and Antarctica forming a continent totaling almost one third of the planet surface. By 700 million years back there were splits developing in the land mass, and fingerlike seas of the increasingly saline waters providing propitious conditions for the implantation of life."

"Our lesson to this point was presented by a Life Carrier once a member of the implantation corps and till now a resident observer."

Lieu 'Life Establishment on Earth' "600 million years ago a commission of Life Carriers arrived to study conditions and locations preparatory to launching a new evolutionary life implanting. The atmosphere at first contained abundant carbon dioxide, but very little oxygen—suitable for plants but not yet animals. Our atmosphere currently extends outward about 400 miles, but actually half of it is packed within the first three miles."

"That we are called Life Carriers should not be misleading—we do carry life to planets, but in the case of earth we brought no life; what we brought 550 million years back were the dossiers of formulation instructions and actual formulas to start life, and that we did in three locations: the eastern or Australasian; the central or Eurasian-African; and the western or Greenland-American locales. So, about 500 million years ago marine vegetable life was well established."

"About 450 million years back the transition from vegetable to animal life took place, and in this case as in such later transformations, missing links have not been found because they never existed—such changes do not evolve as the result of accumulating small changes; they appear full-fledged and suddenly. It is true that small adaptive accommodations do occur, but it happens mostly in response to external alterations that prompt adaptive adjustments."

"The early times of earth's story fall into five eras:

1. Pre-life, archeozoic, 450 million yrs
2. Life-dawn, proterozoic, 150 million yrs
3. Marine-life, Paleozoic, 250 million yrs
4. Land-life Mesozoic, 100 million yrs
5. Mammal-life, enozoic, 50 million yrs. So 400 million yrs back marine life is worldwide, climate is milder,

and continents have given ground to more expansive oceans."

Lieu "250 million years ago the first vertebrate fish arrived, by way of several types of arthropods. Elevation of the continents continued, and oxygen became more plentiful in the atmosphere, and 100 hundred foot ferns were common."

"210 million years back warm-water arctic seas covered much of North America and Europe, and this time was known as the age of frogs. Soon after this the insects appeared, and spiders, scorpions, cockroaches; crickets were abundant— dragon flies were thirty inches across. Sharks dominated the oceans. For 25 million years the great coal deposits formed; some became eighteen thousand feet deep, coal being water- preserved, pressure-modified cellulose."

"180 million years ago came the close of the carboniferous period. Eastern America and Europe were still connected by Greenland, with a more continental climate replacing the previous mild marine climatic conditions. 170 million years back there were sinking ocean beds, and much crust folding into isolated mountain chains. Two new climatic factors emerged in newly raised land masses, glaciation and aridity. Seed plants appeared at this time, and colder weather and dryness led to suspended animation among an increasing variety of animal life. The biological importance of the seas started to diminish—the land was ready."

"150 million years ago North America separates from Asia, but the Bering Strait land bridge does emerge again to close the gap. 140 million years back the fully formed scaled reptiles suddenly arose, yielding crocodiles and similar types, some marine, and some capable of flight in air. Reptilian egg-laying dinosaurs soon became the monarchs of this age, the earlier types being carnivorous, smaller, and bipedal in locomotion. They had hollow avian bones, which became more massive in the later herbivorous types, with a quadruped movement, but all of them differed most markedly from any other creatures then and since, in having a pitifully small brain to body index, which was to become their downfall."

"120 million years ago the dinosaurs and ichthyosaurs were becoming so huge, so sluggish, and such ravenous mechano monsters, that they eventually, by 60 million years back, ate themselves into a blind alley of starvation, and not having the wits to adapt, just disappeared from the face of the earth."

"90 million years ago the angiosperm land plants suddenly arose, and spread over the continents in abundance, as did flowering plants 65 million years back. 55 million years ago a major event took place, the first of the true birds springing into mid-air, directly from the reptilian group, and it prospered. And therewith came the end of the Mesozoic era. And then there arose a true placental mammal, from a small, highly active, carnivorous, springing type of dinosaur, which had persisted in surviving the demise of all its many relatives."

Lieu 'The Age of Early Mammals' "50 million years ago, after a tepid and poor showing of some nonplacental attempts, a true mammal appeared."

"And true mammals: have well developed offsping; which they care for and sustain; with warmblooded agility; using brains superior in size and design."

Lieu 'The Mammalian Era on Earth' "50 million years ago mammalian life was evolving rapidly, mostly in smaller forms, fit to live among the tree tops. They grew two sets of teeth, but no modern types as such had emerged as yet."

"35 million years back marks the beginning of the placental mammalian world domination, and at that time there was considerable renovation and expansion, with brains and agility coming in at a premium. Several groups of mammals took origin in a carnivore now extinct, resembling a cross between a cat and a seal; it was at home on land or in water, was very active and highly intelligent. Early types of the dog family emerged in Europe. Gnawing rodents appeared as well.

"30 million years ago most mammals had preferred mountainous wooded areas, but suddenly hoofed and grazing species appeared on flatter and grassed expanses, with the horse claiming areas in both North America and in Europe. Camels and llamas overran the western plains of the northern Americas, but later the llamas trekked to South America, and the camels to Europe. Also in North America the ancestor of the early lemurs first arose. A group of land mammals took to the seas at this time, developing into whales, dolphins, porpoises, seals, and sea lions. In about ten million years most modern species were established, in at least an ancestral form of those that have survived to later times."

"20 million years back the Bering Strait land bridge allowed the passage of mastodons, rhinoceroses, and many strains of cats from Asia to the Americas. Deer, oxen, and bisons also emerged on the great plains and in the mountains of North America. Huge elephants soon overran the entire world except Australia, and they had the needed larger brains to remain successful. 15 million years ago central Asia produced a common ancestor of the gorilla and a primitive monkey."

# Chapter 13

## From Planet Prince to very Devil

Lieu "Ten million years back all the land on earth was again joined, except Australia, and some notable animal migrations took place: Asiatic sloths, bears, armadillos, and antelopes entered N.America; camels went to Asia. Mastodons went everywhere except to Australia. Five million years ago the true horse left N. America, following the mastodons. Africa finally separated from S.America, and henceforth east was east and west was west, and the Pliocene put paid to that, with no man yet in sight—simians and primates notwithstanding."

"Two million years ago a N.American glacier started moving south. An ice age was in the making, this being the first of six such distinct ice invasions."

Lieu 'Primitive Man in the Ice Age' "One million years back, slightly to the west of India on land now under water, among offspring of the older N.American lemurs, the dawn mammals suddenly appeared. They walked mostly on their hind legs, and had large brains for such small creatures."

"In their seventieth generation a new group suddenly differentiated, the mid mammals, almost twice the size of their forebears. Unexpectedly both simian and primate stock split off at this time, and later from the latter group the first two humans were born. As was meet, our earth was registered as an inhabited world. This was about the time of the third ice age, and to this day it is the Eskimos, the sole survivors of this aboriginal pair, who prefer a cold north."

Lieu 'The men of Color, the Planetary Prince' "500,000 years ago, at the time of the fifth glaciation, two events of grave import occurred: in one generation the six colored races of men mutated from the aboriginal stock; and two, this was the time of the arrival of the Planetary Prince."

Lieu 'The Lucifer Rebellion' "200,000 years back as the sixth and last ice age gathered strength, and before it created the mid continental N.American Great Lakes system, a further calamity descended from the heavens, which became known as the Lucifer Rebellion. Also, at the end of this ice age, about 35,000 years ago, arrived a Material Son and Daughter, inaugurating the Adamic dispensation which would end with the Christ Michael adjudication of its sleeping survivors, of which we spoke some time ago."

Lieu 'Lemurs, Dawn Mammals, Mid Mammals, Primates, Humans' "We should spend some time fleshing out the salient features of this progression."

Erin "An anthropomorphic intrusion, even before the monkeys made man."

Lieu "Relax, my friend, your time will come, will come, will come—you may yet have opportunity to improve on my narration when you yourself go forth and set up some peripatetic garden of edenites."

Erin "I should be so lucky. And where would you be, then, astride my very pineal gland, directing my every syllable with sesquipedalian abstrusions to no academic end? And how would I even know it? Have you noticed that in these latter times you do not even cast a shadow?" Lieu "No, I have not."

Lieu 'The Early Lemurs' "These lemurs evolved from the western or American life implantation, but this strain was reinforced by contributions from the central or African source before further evolution towards human stock took place. The early lemurs migrated by the Bering land bridge and reached the lands to the west of India, where they mixed with favorable strains originally started in Africa. A degree of isolation was achieved by a sinking of the land southwest of the peninsula, and the bulwarks of the glaciers to the north, resulting in an idyllic arena for the cleaving off of two groups, the simian strain on one hand, and the primate-to-human strain on the other."

Lieu 'The Dawn Mammals' "The primate group gave rise to the Mesopotamian dawn mammals, about three feet tall and carnivorous. They had a grasping big toe, and a primitively opposable thumb—the toe would later degenerate but the thumb would slowly but surely specialize to become more versatile and stronger. The dawn mammals were mature at three to four years, with a life span of about twenty. Single births were normal, but occasionally a set of twins was born. They learned how to build good shelters in the tree tops. They made little distinction between warring and hunting and were the dominant life form in this area for one thousand years."

Lieu 'The Mid Mammals' "And it came to pass that a pair of twins were born, male and female, with somewhat less hair, and they grew to be four feet tall, with longer legs and shorter arms, and larger brains. They walked steadily upright. They mated with each other, and produced twenty-one offspring. Mistakes were made, and conflicts worsened, and in time every member of the mid mammals were killed, and for fifteen thousand years the mid mammals were the dominant form of life in their sheltered arena. In a way they were too dominant as their numbers could not be supported by existing resources. They warred until only one hundred survivors remained, a number small enough to remain stable."

Lieu 'The Primates' "Some time passed once more, and two sets of twins were born, one pair to be the ancestors of the apes, the other, already strongly bipedal, and five feet tall, were forerunners to humans. They largely abandoned tree life, matured at about ten years, and lived till they were forty. And these were to be the parents, some 990 thousand years ago, to a first pair of human beings."

Lieu 'The First Human Beings' "With perfectly human thumbs, and feet quite suitable for running, but with toes that could not grasp anything—these twins were walkers and runners. They matured at twelve years and lived to be seventy-five. By the age of ten they worked out an improved language of almost a hundred ideas. With the approving observation of the Life Carriers they decided to migrate northwards, leaving all their relatives behind. The seven adjutant mind spirits could at last make a significant contribution, endowing intuition, and then understanding, courage with a self consciousness, knowledge, counsel, worship, and wisdom. All waited with pent-up anticipation for the full flowering of all these positive, educative instillations to result in full fledged will creatures on earth."

Lieu "It was just 903,408 years back, (from AD 1934) that earth was recognized as a planet of human habitation in the local universe, and a message was received from Lucifer bidding the main body of Life Carriers to return to their home worlds, in recognition of their mission being accomplished."

"An archangel message was received at this time, closing with the words: 'Man mind has appeared on 606 of Satania, and these parents of the new race shall be called Andon and Fonta.' The two did not become aware of these names until the occasion of their fusion with their Father fragments. Strange to relate, the two were definitely superior to many of their immediate descendants, and it was partly their being the first to experience personality that made them feel it advisable to separate themselves from their kin, and migrate north, far away."

"In two years Fonta bore a son, and he was the first primate to be wrapped in animal skin at birth. They had nineteen children, and after some time, fifty grand-children and eventually six great grandchildren. The couple lived to the age of forty-two, when both were killed by the fall of an overhanging rock. The larger group stayed intact until the twentieth generation, when competition and limited resources led to an inevitable dispersion."

"The Andonic tribes were the early river dwellers of France; they lived along the river Somme for tens of thousands of years. They became a superstitious people, turning to the totem worship of various animals, the images of which can still be found on rock walls and in ritualistic carvings. A sacrificial procedure was also developed, with veneration of the animal body becoming part of the belief syndrome—this turned into the first form of sacrifice as an integral part of worship, which Moses later elaborated in the Hebrew ritual, and even became a part of Paul's thinking in the doctrine of atonement for sin by the shedding of blood. A spiritual leader of note arose among the Andonites, named Onagar, (983,323 years before 1934) who taught monotheism, and sent forth his teachers to the far flung tribes to instill a better style of organized government, the most civilized to arise before the coming of the Planetary Prince. It was not until the time of Onagar that guardian seraphim and Father fragments came in greater numbers to the earth—it was the golden age of primitive man."

"Andon and Fonta, shortly after they achieved morontia status in their rapid ascendant progression after mortal death, requested permission that they be stationed indefinitely on the first of the mansion worlds, so they could be there to welcome the ascendant pilgrims from earth. That wish was granted. So you see, Erin, chances are quite good that you will actually meet those two trail blazers."

Erin "That is interesting. But would I be able to understand what they might say?" Lieu "Good question. Consider this: they also requested they might send greetings to earthlings in connection with this revelation, and the response was negative. But had it been positive, you can imagine that along with all the rest of this material, it would have been a small matter to put their message into our English, right?" "Of course. And they could have that help on hand, there."

Lieu 'Early Man' "The Foxhall people in the west were the first humans to live in the England area, and they eventually gave rise to the Eskimo. To the east a branch of Andonites flourished in the hills northwest of India, and this group was the only one not to practice human sacrifice. 850,000 years ago they began a war of extermination against their inferior neighbors, and the resulting long term improvement in the Andonite stock led to the establishment of the Neanderthals, who dominated lands from India to France, to northern Africa, and to China for almost half a million years. The fourth and fifth glaciations were burdensome to them, and they retrogressed to a stage somewhat below that of the Andonites."

Lieu 'The Colored Races' "About 500,000 years ago a couple living in the highlands northeast of India produced a family of unusually intelligent children who, moreover, exhibited a propensity towards strange coloration of the skin: of the 19 children were five red, two orange, four yellow, two green, four blue, and two indigo. So one family, the Sangiks, gave rise to six colored races, as the new colors proved dominant in the offspring of matings with the natives in the area."

"This was most extraordinary—on most evolutionary worlds the red man lives long before succeeding colored primitives arise, and all six races roam the planet long before will creatures evolve: The Sangiks were late; the Andonites early."

Lieu 'Caligastia, the Planetary Prince' "On most planets the arrival of a planetary prince is more or less coincident with the first presence of human will, but on earth the prince came half a million years after Andon and Fonta. He was accompanied by hosts of celestial beings, and by a hundred rematerialized volunteer citizens of advanced ascendant status, each from a different planet, but none from earth. Two resident Life Carriers received authorization to use the life plasm of selected members of the Andonites to reconstitute material bodies for the Caligastia One Hundred, fifty males, and fifty females. These transactions, especially the literal creation of special bodies for the new staff members, gave rise to numerous legends, many of which became confused with the later traditions concerning the planetary installation of Adam and Eve."

"The prince's headquarters was in the Persian Gulf area, enclosed within a forty foot brick wall. It was the norm for the one hundred physical staff to pro-create at about the time when Adam and Eve were expected. They were without Father fragments, these having withdrawn for the duration before the start of this mission, even though the hosts were graduates of the mansion worlds. They were thus definitely superhuman beings. In the thirty-third year of their sojourn, even before the completion of the high walls, it was found that a liaison between one pair resulted in the appearance of the first of the primary midwayers; visible to their staff associates, but not to the human tribes. The Prince now gave leave for the one hundred to procreate at will, and the usual number of 50,000 primary midwayers thus became helpers in the project of fostering the greater well being of such of the human inhabitants who could be persuaded to partake of that opportunity. It was, for the earthlings, the first major encounter with 'spirits'."

Lieu 'The Tree of Life' "A young shrub had come with the Planetary Prince, and when it matured into a tree, the fruit it produced enabled the material and otherwise mortal members of the prince's staff, such as the Andonites who had contributed of their life plasm to the One Hundred (and who had received from the Life Carriers the required alterations to benefit from the system circuits,) to live on indefinitely on earth, so long as they ate the fruit as part of their diet."

Lieu 'Curriculum of the Prince's School'

"1. Food and material welfare—well digging, irrigation, skin handling, weaving; cooking, drying, and smoking food.

2. Animal care—selection, domestication, breeding; transport, with and without wheeled contrivances, soil cultivation; making butter and cheese; carrier pigeon messaging.

3. Safety from predators—the mighty wall, superior dwellings, night fires, various traps and movement controls.

4. Use and conservation of general knowledge—25 character alphabet and its use in writing, but the hopes for one language and culture was lost with the Lucifer rebellion.

5. Industry and Trade—many goods, notably salt, spices, and tools were bartered, and tokens were used for credits and other contractual arrangements.

6. Religion and Worship—Of note: 'The Father's Prayer' which encanted thus: "Father of all, whose Son we honor, look down upon us with favor. Deliver us from the fear of all, save you. Make us a pleasure to our

divine teachers and forever put truth on our lips. Deliver us from violence and anger; give us respect for our elders and for that which belongs to our neighbors. Give us this season green pastures and fruitful flocks to gladden our hearts. We pray for the hastening of the coming of the uplifter, and we would do your will on this world as others do on worlds beyond."

7.  Health and Survival—the benefits of cooking, boiling, and roasting in forestalling illness and contamination; the burning of refuse and the burial of decomposing rubbish for hygienic controls; the blessing of sunlight in avoiding fungus and other harmful infections; the use of bathing and cleansing was advised, with religious approval as a constant encouragement.

8.  Art and Science—the working of metals with the aid of fire was taught, and the plastic arts were fostered, especially the shaping and baking of clay sculptures.

9.  Tribal relations—a form of statehood developed and courtship and marriage were promoted and standardized; competitive games were invented and refined, though humor was not common with primitives.

10. A supreme council, headed by Van promoted rule-following and standard semi-legal adherence to formal agreements and contractual arrangements—it was a good start, reinforced by the sevenfold code called 'The Father's Way':

    1.  "You shall not fear nor serve any God but the Father of all.

2. You shall not disobey the Father's Son, our world's ruler nor disrespect his superhuman associates.
3. You shall not speak a lie when called before the judges.
4. You shall not kill men, women, or children.
5. You shall not steal your neighbor's goods or cattle.
6. You shall not touch your friend's wife.
7. You shall not disrespect your parents nor the elders of the tribe."

"This was the law of the Prince's domain for 300,000 years, until the Caligastia betrayal in the Lucifer Rebellion." "Here ends chapter 13, by a Melchizedek"

Lieu 'The Caligastia Betrayal' "At the end of the peaceful time in the prince's domain, when 300,000 years of steady progress were secured, Satan came on one of his periodic inspection visits, and he told Caligastia of the already determined stance taken by Lucifer, and the upcoming 'Declaration of Liberty'. Caligastia forthwith cast his lot with the rebellion, forsaking his place of trust and his calling to lead the people on earth in their course to ascenscion."

"Error obtains with a misconception of reality. Evil is a maladjustment to universe reality. Sin is a purposeful resistance to divine reality, a conscious choosing to oppose spiritual progress. Iniquity consists in an open and defiant stance in such denial of all reality as to impair personality integrity, resulting in borderline cosmic insanity."—"Caligastia chose to embrace all four, and he has become, in the minds of the very earthlings he came here to inspire that they might become princes of mortal ascenders, an apostate prince, nay, the devil himself, and is as that very devil memorialized in the Holy Scriptures."

Lieu 'Van rebels vs Caligastia' "The Prince directed his chief lieutenant, Daligastia, to proclaim to the ten councils of administration, that they all should abdicate, as Caligastia was on the point of proclaiming himself the sole absolute sovereign of earth, and as such would redistribute all administrative authority as he might see fit in due course. But Van, the leader of Council Ten, declared this to be planetary rebellion, and appealed to all the councils'staff that they postpone any response until Lucifer were consulted, and he won their consent."

"However, the appeal to Lucifer resulted in their being instructed to comply. Van delivered a masterful oratory of dissent, speaking for seven hours straight, and there ensued a relentless standoff for seven long years following—the core of the staff remaining true to the unseen Father."

# Chapter 14

## Andonite to SonGod to Midway

Lieu 'Loyalists Dwell Apart' "Upon everyone making the portentous choice, the loyal cherubim and seraphim, and three loyal midwayers assumed the custody of the tree of life, permitting only their loyal companions, which included fifty-six of the modified Andonites, to partake of the fruit and leaves."

"During the time of this rift the loyalists withdrew, taking the precious tree to an unwalled and poorly sheltered area some miles to the east. The site and tree were guarded day and night by the midwayers. And so it was for seven years."

"Forty of the One Hundred remained loyal, and sixty rebelled, and chose Nod as their leader. The sixty soon realized some of what they had lost in that they no longer had hopes of immortality, so in spite of being instructed to procreate at will, upon the fall of the prince's headquarters, they withdrew to become known as Nodites, living in 'the land of Nod'. These events gave some impetus to the legends of the gods coming down to mate with the daughters of men."

"In the relations of the Prince's followers with the untaught Andonites farther afield, things soon went from civil to cavil, and years before the sinking of this area beneath the waves 160 years after the rebellion, the primitives lay waste to the headquarter 'city,' so that its end was very much worse than its beginning."

"Van was the trustworthy leader of the loyalist group for ages, the titular head of all superhuman personalities for 150,000 years, right to the time of Adam. He was in the meantime ably assisted by twelve Melchizedek receivers, two resident Life Carriers, a volunteer Teacher Son, and a director general of angelic beings."

"Within 1,000 years of the rebellion, Van had 350 outposts of civilization flourishing in promising locations among the native Andonite settlements."

Lieu 'The Genesis of War' "Before the partial socialization of the advancing races man was exceedingly individualistic, extremely suspicious, and doubtless unbelievably quarrelsome. Violence is the law of nature, hostility the automatic reaction of its children, while war is but the same activity done collectively."

"War is the natural state and heritage of evolving man; peace is the yardstick of his advancement in the attainment of civilization. The Andonites were early taught the golden rule, and even today their Eskimo descendants live very much by that code; custom is strong among them—they are fairly free from violence."

Lieu 'Material Sons—Adam and Eve' "Although the people surviving on earth in these ancient times were culturally and spiritually compromised by the effects of the Lucifer rebellion, biologic evolution was not much impaired and so, about 50,000 years ago the Life Carriers of the realm submitted a petition asking that two material sons, racial uplifters, be sent to earth, and this was granted."

"Some 83 years before Adam and Eve arrived, Van recruited three thousand volunteers to prepare for their coming, starting with the location of a good area for the needed Garden of Eden. In three years, the best site was agreed to be a peninsula jutting west from the far end of the Mediterranean, and the next two years were devoted to the removal of all amenities, including the tree of life, from the loyalist areas to that location."

Lieu 'The Garden of Eden' "Animal husbandry would be tended to in an enclosed area of the mainland, and a brick wall was built across the isthmus to separate the Garden proper from that space."

"Counting back from the year 1934, Adam and Eve arrived 37,848 years ago, and they regained consciousness in their newly recreated bodies simultaneously ten days after landing. They were a little more than eight feet tall."

"At the time of their selection they were engaged in trial and testing physical laboratory research, but before that they had been for fifteen thousand years directors of the division of experimental energy in its application to the trial modification of living forms. When they left for earth they bid their goodbyes to fifty sons and fifty daughters. Both Adam and Eve were well versed in the language spoken by Van and his associates, and it was a great surprise to the earthlings to hear their new masters address them in their earthly tongue."

"The Material Sons spent the first six days exploring their surroundings, meeting the people and reviewing the animal stocks and the state of agriculture, and on the seventh day they rested, but led a noontide ceremony of thanksgiving. And thus was born the Sabbath Day, which continues to grace us even now."

"One reason the Edenites were moved to regard Adam and Eve as gods was the fact that the two gave forth a shimmer of light, some of which escaped the clothes they wore. This light effect was quite obvious about their heads, and this gave rise to the tradition of representing pious and holy individuals as having a halo over the head. Another thing that made the material sons seem godlike was the fact that they were able to communicate with each other, and with their children, over a distance of some fifty miles, a phenomenon we now would call telepathy, although in their case it turned out to be dependent on spiritual clarity, as it ceased to function when the two started to heed the dicta of Caligastia."

"The first-born of Adam and Eve was named Adamson, the second a daughter, and the third the son named Eveson— they were the original members of the violet race. Eve gave birth to sixty-three children before the default, about evenly split between daughters and sons. At the time of leaving the Garden there were four generations, comprising 1,647 pure-line descendants."

"There was no cooking in Adam's household: fruits, nuts and cereals were harvested and cared for to be ready to eat without any special treatment, and no milk was used from any of the animals; in addition to benefits of the tree of life there was also a direct access to certain energy-bearing space emanations for those who could profit thereby. They ate just once a day, around noontime."

"Maturity was attained at age eighteen, and that was the accepted time of betrothal, which was followed by a two year course of instruction preparatory to marriage and a lifework if applicable. Since the plan was to have their numbers grow to around a million, siblings had to mate with each other, and this practice had its effect on the mating customs of later royalty whose members, supposedly descended from the gods, were accorded similar license."

Lieu 'A Creation Story' "The Hebrews had no general written language till long after they reached Palestine, when ca 900 B.C. they learned an alphabet from the Philistines. They had several stories of creation at hand, but they inclined to a modified Mesopotamian version. Their traditions crystallized about Moses, who made shrift to trace a lineage from Abram back to Adam, and so it was simply assumed that Adam was the first man, and his unique six days were credited to the timespan of the earth's creation. And so, a thousand years after the life of Moses the story of the creation in six days was written out and the account of it credited to Moses. Ptolemy, sovereign of Egypt, had this translated into Greek and placed in his library in Alexandria. So it forms part of the Christian canon."

Lieu 'The Adamic Default' "Before the Melchizedeks left they had warned Eve to be careful not to be led astray by the wily Caligastia, and she followed their advice for one hundred years, but the difficulties of the uplift program and its lack of success thus far in improving the lot of the changeable and less than noble Andonites led to her hardly noticing that there could be cause for concern in the attentions of a Nodite leader called Serapatatia, whose visits she appreciated more and more as a welcome diversion, and when he proposed, shortly after becoming the leader of the Syrian Nodites to form a closer association with the Edenites to the end that such collaboration would help the material sons in their project of social, moral, and spiritual progression of all the

surrounding races, both Adam and Eve were very pleased—
Serapatatia was a powerful, engaging and intelligent leader.
And he did not even suspect that Caligastia was actively and
constantly whispering suggestions to his below conscious
musings, feeding his growing fascination with Eve, and when
Serapatatia conceived the plan to give the whole uplifting
campaign a perfect boost by arranging for a violet-race leader
of the Nodites to take special charge of the whole project,
Eve listened. For five years these secret plans were quietly
matured, and one fateful night she took a most notable and
attractive Nodite leader of a neighboring tribe, named Cano,
to her bed and received the seed that would become the living
Cain."

"The celestial life of the planet was astir, and Adam
recognized that something was wrong—he asked Eve to
come aside with him in the Garden. As they communed in
the moonlit night the 'voice in the garden' reproved them for
their disobedience. Eve had told Cano of the oft-repeated
warning against modifying the divine plan, which was worded:
'In the day that you commingle good and evil, you shall surely
become as mortals of the realm; you shall surely die', but
Cano, accustomed to the casual relations between men and
women outside the Garden, assured her that if this were done
from worthy motives it could do no evil, and that she would live
on in the person of their child. Eve's disillusion was pathetic."

"Adam was heartbroken and dejected. The next day he
sought out Laotta, the brilliant Nodite woman who was head
of the western schools of the Garden, and with premeditation,
chose to share Eve's fate—the thought of a lonely vigil on

earth without Eve was more than he could endure. The die was cast: the Default was complete."

Lieu 'A War Party' "When they heard what had happened to Eve, the Edenites were furious, and before anything could be done to restrain them they rushed out and destroyed the Nodite settlement, killing everyone, including Cano. Serapatatia, devastated, drowned himself. Adam, totally distraught, went off into the woods, and wandered aimlessly for thirty days. He returned, chastened and sad, but resolved that it was time to take counsel and plan for the future. Wars and rumor of wars arose. The story of the destruction of the Nodite settlement reached other tribes, and presently a great host was assembling to march on the Garden. Until long after the Edenites left to found the second Garden there was bitter warfare between them and the Nodites. Adam had no taste for warfare and resolved to leave the Garden to the Nodites unopposed."

"Seventy days after Eve's dereliction the Melchizedek receivers returned to earth and assumed jurisdiction over world affairs again, but they had been cautioned against involving themselves with the Adamites in any direct manner."

"On the third day out from the Garden, the journey was halted by the arrival of seraphic transports and Gabriel, for the purpose of settling what would become of the material sons' offspring. All children of prechoice age were removed; of those who were twenty or older two thirds chose to depart, and the remainder stayed with their parents. Gabriel explained to the parents that although they had not been judged to be in rebellion, or in contempt of the universe government, the very act of contravening the terms of their mission brought an automatic stay and cessation of their immortality—they would not be supported by the spirit gravity of the Infinite Spirit, and would henceforth glean no benefit from the tree of life."

Lieu 'The Fall of Man' "The impairment of the Adamic mission did result in a less than planned benefit to the human races, but the earthlings did not fall—there was not a Fall of Man in this sense. Caligastia's interference caused Adam and Eve to accomplish less than had been their expected goal, and mankind did not get the fuller upsurge in biologic improvement as did races on other planets."

"The journey to the Euphrates, which had been one of the three sites chosen for the first Garden, was not yet complete when both Eve and Laotta gave birth. Laotta died in childbirth, so Eve took the daughter, Sansa, to her bosom and cared for her as well as for Cain. The soil between the two rivers had not been prepared, so it was here that the Adamites had to prepare the ground for proper cultivation, 'in the sweat of their brow'. In less than two years Abel was born, and the story of the brother dispute is familiar to the readers of scripture. Cain had been defiant of the family traditions, and disdainful of Adam's religion, but after the death of Abel it became apparent Cain would have to leave the family hearth and seek his fortune elsewhere. He took serious counsel with Eve, and at this juncture he took the step to moral/spiritual acceptance needed for the Father fragment's full indwelling, which had heretofore not come about. Cain went to the land of Nod, and married Remona, his distant cousin, and the two promoted peace between their peoples. Their first son, Enoch, became the head of the Elamite Nodites and peace did indeed prevail."

Lieu 'The Seth Priesthood' "The oldest son born in the second garden was Seth, and he instituted the line of religious rulers, whose duties were three-fold: religion, health, and education. They were missionaries to the Andonites."

"The Material Sons and their offspring were the violet race, with blue eyes, fair complexions, and light colored hair varying over yellow, red, and brown."

"Adam and Eve lived about 500 years. Eve passed on first, of a weakened heart, and Adam of general functional failure some nineteen years later. They were buried under the floor of the central temple, and this led to a custom that survived until modern times, that spiritual notables be interred in this manner."

"Adam and Eve came to earth as Sons of God; they left it as man and woman, with the usual characteristics of other mortals of the earth—ascendant aspirants, sons of man." "Was it Paul who spoke of Jesus as the Second Adam?"

"Here ends this section, much of which was presented by Solonia,

the seraphic 'voice in the Garden'."

Lieu 'The Midwayers' "The midway creatures function on a level about halfway or midway between the mortals of a planet and the angels. The primary group originate with the coming of a planetary prince; the secondary with that of the Material Sons. Remember, a supermaterial (nonsexual) liaison of a male and a female of the corporeal staff resulted in the first-born of the primary midwayers, and the rest of 50,000 followed in due course, so one thousand were born to each couple, and that limit proved to be binding. A good 40,000 defected to Lucifer."

"About 35,000 B.C. Adamson, aged 120, went to one of the easternmost Vanite centers to found a new hub of civilization. His mate and their children had all

elected to join the prechoice children in the seraphic transports, so he was more or less a lost soul, looking for new roots. He was, however, accompanied by twenty-seven kindred spirits, and they found the settlement he had dreamt of."

# Chapter 15

## The Path of Moses

"It was here he found Ratta, a beauty of twenty, who claimed to be the last pure-line descendant of the Prince's staff. She had decided not to wed, but Adamson was the perfect solution, in person. In three months they were married, and went on to have sixty-seven children, but a strange thing—every fourth child was often invisible. The two parents were, after all, partly superhuman."

"Ratta was perturbed, but Adamson remembered the primary midwayers and correctly surmised that this development was of a similar order. When the first male-female pair were ready, he encouraged them to marry, thus initializing the secondary order of midwayers, and within one hundred years, about two thousand secondary midway creatures were brought into being."

"At the death of Adamson thirty-three of these went over in a body to join the primary midwayers in the service of the Melchizedeks, but the others became an unorganized and irregular group of mischief makers, some of whom were partially brought under control by Machiventa Melchizedek when Abram was active, but it was not until Jesus came that the majority of them swung over to join the primary midwayers. Both orders of midway creatures which did not join the Lucifer rebellion are still on earth, about 1100 of the secondary ones."

"They are nonmaterial beings as regards nutrition and energy intake, and do not sleep nor procreate, but they partake of many human traits, and enjoy humor and will join in worship. When attached to mortals they enter into the spirit of human work, rest, and play. They are nearer men than angels, and are invaluable to seraphim serving as personal guardians."

"Of the two groups it is the primary one that is closer to the angels, and their activities and services more typically involve spiritual and angelic activities. It is the secondary midwayers who are usually closer to people, in nature and in their affinities, coming just outside the range of human vision, and having definite powers over time-space material things and creatures of the realm. Their chief work today is that of unperceived personal-liaison associates of the planetary reserve corps of destiny, and they have played a significant part in the realization of the revelation of which this lesson is a part. They do not ordinarily permit humans to witness their actions, or to see them."

Erin "Ah hah, now I've got you! After all our talk about who/what you actually are, and all your dodging around, we've finally got it—you are a secondary mid-wayer, you are! Well, what about it? What have you got to say about that?"

Lieu "Well Erin, what have I said before? You know very well—I have said that I do not know, and I've said that I cannot say. Why do you now assume that just because I have told you some things about secondary midwayers that sound a bit familiar, you can just jump up and declare that I am such a creature? Is it logical, sensible, scientific? I don't know; I cannot say." Erin "Bloody hell!" Lieu "Quite!"


Lieu "At the last adjudication of this world when Michael removed the slumbering survivors, the midwayers were left behind—they now function as a single corps, The United Midwayers of Earth, embracing both orders, and number nearly 11,000 members. Midwayers are anchored on a planet until it graduates as settled in light and life, and from birth on they learn, grow, and evolve to become greater and increasingly perfect in all significant arenas. There are many great minds and mighty spirits among them."

"Generations of men forget; midwayers remember, and store a treasure house of all the better traditions—even as the story of the life and teachings of Jesus has been given by them to their cousins in the flesh."

Lieu 'The Violet Race after Adam' "The chief center of Adamite culture was in the second garden, in the triangle of the Tigris and Euphrates. The secondary was the Adamsonite center, east of the southern shore of the Caspian Sea."

Lieu 'The Sumerians' "A small group of Nodites at the mouth of these two rivers maintained their racial integrity for thousands of years, and eventually blended with Adamites to found the Sumerian peoples of historic times, 200,000 years after the sinking of the Garden, and their language was more Aryan than." Lieu 'Lake Van, Mt Ararat, Assyrians, Babel' "Northern Nodites and Vanites arose prior to the Babel conflict, and settled near Lake Van, close to Mt Ararat which became their sacred mountain. 10,000 years ago the Vanite ancestors of the Assyrians taught that their seven moral commandments had been given Van by the Gods on Mt Ararat, and that Van and Amadon translated there alive."

"At about this time 375 members from the second Adamsonite center made their way to Greece, and they carried the most valuable strains of the emerging white races—they were of a high order intellectually and physically. The art and genius of these people were the legacy of Adamson and his extraordinary second wife, a direct descendant of the Nodite staff of Prince Caligastia. With Adam, Adamson, Ratta, and this latest remarkable super-lady, no wonder the Greeks had traditions of being descendants of gods and superhuman heroes."

"The Adamites were a real nation around 19,000 BC, numbering 4.5 million, who had already contributed millions of their progeny to surrounding peoples. About 15,000 BC most of them ended up in Europe and central Asia."

"About 2500 BC the Sumerian capital Lagash fell, and when Hammurabi ruled, the Sumerians had been absorbed by northern Semites, and were no more."

Lieu 'Noah and the Ark' "There has never been a universal flood since life began on earth: the Biblical story of Noah and the Flood is an invention of the Hebrew priesthood during the Babylonian captivity. Noah, however, was a real person: he was a winemaker of Aram, a river settlement near Erech. He kept track of water levels in the river, and was wont to warn people to build their houses out of wood, boat style, and to put family animals inside overnight when the waters rose. He built himself a robust houseboat, and one fateful year the flood was so great that few besides his household survived. The houseboat saved them."

Lieu 'Prayer and the Alter Ego' "Children, when first learning to speak, are prone to say their thoughts in words. With the dawn of creative imagination they may converse with imaginary companions, so that a budding ego communes with a fictitious alter ego. One step further and a pseudo dialogue develops in which the alter ego replies to the child's commentary."

"In time the alter ego is exalted to the status of divine dignity, and prayer as an agency of religion begins to manifest itself as the conservation of the highest values and ideals of those who pray. Prayer, then, at any of these stages, is a socializing, moralizing, and spiritualizing practice. Prayer is a twofold experience: it induces the novice to look for aid to the subconscious body of its own mortal experience—and for guidance and inspiration, to the Father fragment within."

Erin "Alright now, just stop right there for a bit. This account you just recited is a much more persuasive and a much closer fitting suggestion for your genesis and ontology than the one we argued about a while ago."

Lieu "Sorry, I don't know what you mean by that. What I did was to go over a way that talking with an imaginary friend could over time develop into praying, by the child who, growing in age and grace, begins to assign a partly spiritual, a more than human character to the respondent in his semi— imaginary dialogue. And that says nothing about me, nothing added about who or what I am, or was."

Erin "No, it's not as straightforward as that. When I first became aware of you you were definitely an imaginary friend—you spoke to me, to help me in dealing with a hostile dog, and I could not see you. And after that, although you were certainly a friend, you became less and less imaginary, because any time there was no danger or awkwardness in it, I could see you just fine, just like any other person. You became more real, not less, and I mean real as a person: we were practically school buddies, learning things in parallel, and we undertook the exploring of revelation very much in the way of a school project. Right?"

Lieu "Pretty much, yes. But you can see in your summary of these things that I was not going from being an alter ego to being a spiritual one. True, I was more independent and assertive than imaginary friends are wont to be, but the two of us being more inventive in gathering and sharing information about abstruse matters that do not fit very easily into the time-space world of hard reality, does not even suggest that either of us is anything more than unusually imaginative."

Erin "But there is no way you could tell me the tons of material about the universe, and about creation; about the organization of the cosmos; about the trillions of beings totally new to our understanding or any part of our experience, without there being spirituality, or at least a mental reach beyond anything heretofore suspected, that can possibly account for all that."

Lieu "Oh Erin! How can you be so willfully blind. Have you not heard of the strange things that come to people in their dreams, or if you will, their visions?"

Erin "When you tell me all that stuff, neither one of us is dreaming, nor could you be 'dreaming up' what you are telling me." "True, but the question lingers, right where we left it before—I do not know, and I cannot say, I'm sorry."

Lieu 'Machiventa Melchizedek' "With the betrayal of Caligastia, and then the default of Adam and Eve, the twelve Melchizedek receivers became more and more alarmed at the state of affairs in regard to revealed truth on earth; there was a definite erosion of all things sacred, of what had been taught to earthlings. These emergency Sons appealed to the administrative powers at the head of the local and the superuniverse for direction as to what might be done in this matter, but received little encouragement—being told only it was simply up to them."

"Thus it was that Machiventa volunteered to personalize on earth as a man of the realm, that he might bestow himself as an Emergency Son of world ministry, and this plan was put into motion 1,973 years before the birth of Jesus."

"Within a few years, in the area around Salem, he had gathered a group of believers and disciples who later became the nucleus of the city of Jerusalem."

"The sage of Salem had a six foot body, resembling the blended Sumerian and Nodite people, materialized much in the manner in which the One Hundred physical helpers of Caligastia had been, but it did not carry the life plasm of any human race—he could not conceive offspring. He abandoned this body after ninety-four years of service, though it was still hale and whole at that time."

"During his time in the flesh the sage was able to communicate fully with his eleven partner Melchizedeks, but not with any other celestial personalities."

"Machiventa lived for thirty years with the family of Katro, and he taught them more than he did any public gatherings. These teachings were treasured by the host and those close to him, right to the days of their eventual illustrious descendant Moses, including the promise of the coming of another son of God who would be born of woman. This was how it came about that Jesus was regarded as a holy minister 'after the order of Melchizedek'."

Lieu 'The Selection of Abram' "The choice of Palestine as the site for Machiventa's mission was in part determined by the goal of establishing contact with a family showing good potential for leadership, and although the expression 'chosen people' has been less than fortuitous, Abram was certainly a chosen person, and the area in which this Melchizedek and Abram were active was definitely a chosen locale. Abram's father, Terah, and his brother Nahor, were less than enthusiastic about relinquishing the many Mesopotamian household gods, but they had heard of the King of Salem, and left Ur to investigate further."

"A few weeks after the death of Terah a message arrived for Abram and Nahor—'Come to Salem . . . and in the enlightened offspring of you two brothers shall all the world be blessed'. Nahor did not go, but Lot and his uncle Abram did go, and built a stronghold in the hills near the city of Salem."

"Abram had kingly ambitions, and soon attained recognition as the civic ruler of Salem and the surrounding seven tribes, but Machiventa urged him to establish peaceful relations with those farther afield."

Lieu "Abram and Machiventa could not reconcile their difference in this, and Abram relocated to Hebron, where he soon was in a state of war with an eleven tribe confederation that had presumed to make war on Lot at Sodom. Abram won this campaign and, convinced he had been given this victory by support from the God of Machiventa, imposed on the vanquished a tithing arrangement to the benefit of the Salem hegemony. When Abram and Machiventa met in consultation afterwards they formalized an interfaith covenant of mutual goodwill by which Abram's issue would dominate the area of Canaan, and back the Salem settlers."

"Abram, mightily moved by this covenant, had it solemnized by committing it to writing; by changing his name to Abraham; and by being the first of his lineage to submit to circumcision. After this he became the secular manager of affairs for the community of Salem, which gave Machiventa more scope to organize a great campaign of spreading his teachings by sending missionaries in all directions. The Salem teachers penetrated to Egypt, Mesopotamia, and Asia Minor, and later, to all of Europe and England, as well as Iceland, and then to Japan and China."

"Sad to relate, these teachings were too advanced spiritually to supplant the old beliefs which had so long prevailed in all these areas, so in general there was no definite metanoia, only a short-lived recognition that other beliefs existed."

"Shortly after the destruction of Sodom and Gomorrah the bestowal of Machiventa came to an end, as he realized he had accomplished as much as he could reasonably hope for, and as well, his followers were becoming more and more convinced he was himself an instance of divinity, despite his thorough explanations of his proper role among them. To underline this fact, let it be remembered that in many cases where persons of note had discourse with Machiventa, the narration in the Old Testament referenced the latter as God."

"The proselytizing was not all in vain, as it came to pass that in the sixth century before Michael, through an unusual coordination of spiritual agencies not altogether understood by superhuman monitors, from a small number of inspired earthlings, there was a revivifying re-presentation of the Salem truths, as for instance, by the Chinese teachers Lao-Tse and Confucius, the former of the two presenting one of the earliest instances of the doctrine of returning good for evil: 'Goodness begets goodness, but to the one who is truly good, evil also begets goodness' and he viewed life as the emergence of personality from cosmic potentials, which we have encountered in much more detail in this goodspel."

Lieu 'Worship in Tibet' "In Tibet may be found the strangest amalgam of Salem teachings with Buddhism, Hinduism, Taoism, and Christianity—elaborate rituals involve bells, chants, incense, processionals, rosaries, and holy water. They have rigid dogmas, crystallized creeds, mystic rites, and special fasts. This in a hierarchy of monks, nuns, and abbots. They pray to gods, to angels, to saints and a Holy Mother, they practice confession and teach a purgatory. Would that prayer wheels and the plethora of religious bits and pieces might give way to: sonship to God, brotherhood among man, and citizenship of ascending mortals."

Lieu 'The Fateful Moses' "The beginning of the evolution of the Hebraic concept and ideals of a supreme Creator dates from the departure of the Semites from Egypt under the great leader, teacher, and organizer, Moses."

"The slaves he led were a forlorn, downcast, dejected, and ignorant group who hardly had a set of beliefs that might be called religion, yet they were the people from which his father had been selected to mediate between the royal house and the Semite workers, and although Moses' mother was of the royal family, he cast his lot with the slaves, and even saw to it that a number got some education."

"As related in scripture, this band of mostly vagabonds did escape the pharaoh's warriors, and eventually made their way to Mt. Sinai, where Moses presented them with the Ten Commandments. While they were still in the area, his teaching of Yahweh as a more credible god was highlighted by a grand volcanic eruption, presenting the titular Jehovah as a god of quaking mountain, of wrathful all-consuming fire, and an obfuscating smoke—a jealous and implacable god in the image of an vengeful tyrant, beyond reason or rationality."

"There is little on record of the real and lasting work of Moses because the Hebrews at the time of the exodus had no written language—these activities were eventually recorded more than a thousand years after their occurrence."

Erin "No, no,no! It was not like that, not at all. What about the trickery with Moses and the king's magicians? And what about the plagues, and the butchery of the first born sons? Are you forgetting all those things?" Lieu "Erin, I do but give to you just what was given me, as I have always done. If you want, instead of that, to read what is in scripture, be my guest and read it there. I do not make a claim concerning what exactly was or was not—I can only say what I have heard and hear again as I do speak."

# Chapter 16

## Jesus, 16 to 21

Lieu '<u>History Sacred and Profane</u>' "The custom of pronouncing Hebrew experience as sacred history, and all other happenings as history profane has caused endless confusion, confounded to no end by the fact that there is no secular history of the Jews. After the priests of the Babylonian exile had prepared a new record of God's supposedly miraculous dealings with the Hebrews in the Old Testament, they carefully and completely destroyed existing records of Hebrew affairs—such books as 'The Doings of the Kings of Israel' and 'The Doings of the Kings of Judah'."

"It must be remembered that the Jews failed to develop an adequate non-theologic philosophy of life, as they were too long shackled with the Egyptian concepts of divine reward for righteousness, and extreme punishment for sin."

"The pessimism of Ecclesiastes was a worldly-wise reaction against the first of these two errors, and the drama of Job was protest against the second, but neither was effective—false hopes prevailed to such degree Jews recognized neither the reality of the Son of Paradise nor heeded his essential message."

"New Testament authors and later Christian writers augmented the distortion of Hebrew history by a well-meant transcendentalization of the Jewish prophets."

"However, the Jews, through the successive teachers of Israel, actually accomplished the transformation of the barbarically picayune Yahweh of tribal notoriety, into the loving and merciful Father of all mankind, further enlarged and amplified by the teaching and life example of Christ Michael."

Lieu 'Religious Faith' "The soul of man reveals itself by the manner in which it induces the person to react to inevitable trials. The moral consciousness of genuine spiritual faith is in enactment inasmuch as it:

1. Induces ethics and morals to advance despite animalistic tendencies
2. Portrays sublime trust in God's goodness despite adversity or calamity
3. Generates courage and confidence despite adversity or calamity
4. Has inexplicable poise and normally sustains tranquility
5. Maintains composed personality in the face of maltreatment
6. Keeps a faith and trust in ultimate victory in the face of blind fate
7. Has unswerving belief in God despite contrary sophistries
8. Lives in solid triumph despite overly technocratic obfuscation
9. Contributes to the ineluctable onward march of altruism."

Lieu 'Limitations of Revelation' "Mankind should understand that we who participate in the revelation of truth are rigorously held to the instructions that delimit the boundaries prescribed in the applicable mandate authorizing them."

"Further, let it be clear that what we convey is not necessarily inspired—it is limited by our mission for the coordination and sorting of present-day knowledge, and although we are aware of forthcoming developments therein, we may not make that part of our revelation. With our apologies, we must leave it so."

Lieu 'Creator Son to Son of Man' "When a Creator Son, with his helpmate Creative Spirit has completed the building of a local universe, he must, in order to become the unimpeachable sovereign of that universe, undergo a sevenfold series of bestowal endowments. "Christ Michael, almost one billion years ago, enacted a bestowal as a Melchizedek Son, subject to the combined will of the Father, Son, and Spirit, and this experience was completed in one hundred earth years." "About 150 million years afterwards, the second bestowal was undertaken, and Michael existed as a System Sovereign, subject to the will of the Father and the Son, dealing as a Lanonandek Son with local rebellion problems in system eleven of constellation thirty-seven."

"The third bestowal was as a Material Son, subject to the will of the Father and the Spirit, acting as a Planetary Prince of world 217, effecting its reclamation."

"Michael's fourth foray was as a Seraphim, subject to the will of the Son and the Spirit, assigned to a corps of teaching counselors and acting as private secretary to twenty-six master teachers."

"The fifth bestowal, again a stage lower in the scale of existence than the one before, was as an ascendant pilgrim of mortal origin, subject to the will of the Infinite Spirit."

"The sixth bestowal was subject to the will of the Eternal Son, as a morontia mortal of Endantum." "In each of these bestowals Michael had appeared as did Machiventa on earth, a fully mature individual, but next, on his <u>seventh and final bestowal,</u> he would come as an infant of the realm, subject to the will of the Universal Father, as Jesus of Nazareth, son of Mary and Joseph."

Lieu '<u>The Life of Jesus of Nazareth</u>' "The narration that follows was sponsored by a commission of twelve midwayers, under the supervision of a Melchizedek revelatory director. The overall basis was supplied by a secondary midwayer onetime assigned to the watchcare of the Apostle Andrew."

"Just before his departure for his earth incarnation, Michael conferred his local universe administrative responsibilities to the custody of Immanuel."

"Gabriel proposed a study of racial groups on earth, and proposed the Jewish people to Michael as the most propitious choice, and Michael agreed. Then a family commission chose three couples, and Gabriel selected Joseph and Mary."

"The ancestry of Joseph went back to Abraham, along Sumerians, Nodites, and back to Andon and Fonta. David and Solomon were not in the direct line, nor was Adam a member of this succession."

"Mary was of more mixed lineage, including Syrian, Hittite, Phoenician, Greek, and Egyptian—racially considered she was not actually Jewish, although in culture and belief she definitely was."

"Late in June of 8 B.C. Gabriel had appeared to Elizabeth, kin to Mary and wife of the priest Zacharias, and told her she would have a son who would be the fore-runner of the divine teacher to come, son to Mary."

"He appeared to Mary in November of 8 B.C."

Lieu 'Joseph's Dream' "Gabriel's announcement to Mary was made the day following the conception of Jesus, and it was the only supernatural occurrence that in connection with her conceiving and bearing the child of promise."

"At first Joseph had doubts about the Gabriel visitation, until he had a most extraordinary dream, in which a celestial messenger appeared to him, saying: 'Joseph, I appear by command of Him who now reigns on high, and I am directed to say, concerning the son Mary will bear, that he shall be a great light in the world, his life shall become the light of mankind. He shall first come to his own people, but they will hardly receive him; but to as many as shall receive him to them he will reveal that they are the children of god'."

"In these visitations nothing was said about the house of David, nor was anything intimated about Jesus becoming a 'deliverer of the Jews' or that he would be the long-expected Messiah."

"Joseph did later go to Bethlehem, the City of David, to be registered for the Roman census, but this was because six generations previously his paternal ancestor was orphaned, and was adopted by a man named Zadoc, who was of the 'house of David'. Jesus himself later came to the point of publicly denyng any connection with the house of David."

"Joseph and Mary met when Joseph did some work for her father, and after a courtship of two years, when Joseph was twenty-one, in March of 8 B.C. were married at Mary's home, as was the custom of that time and place."

"Joseph held vigorously to the Eastern or Babylonian practices of the Jewish religion—Mary was more inclined to the Western or Hellenistic interpretation. Joseph expected a spiritual teacher son, Mary a nationalistic Messiah."

"Mary and Joseph were well educated for their day and station, and made sure that their children too enjoyed that benefit."

"In the month of March of 8 B.C. another event of great import took place—Caesar Augustus decreed that all inhabitants of the Roman Empire should be numbered for taxation purposes, but in this area, due to difficulties with Herod, king of Judea, the census was not held until one year later, the year 7 B.C."

"Early on the morning of 18 August 7 B.C. Joseph and Mary set off for Bethlehem, and arrived at an inn to spend the night of 20 August 7 B.C. At noon the next day, August 21st, Jesus was born, and was laid in a nearby manger."

"Zacharias and Elizabeth were not far, and as they held the Messianic faith as strongly as Mary did, they all prevailed upon Joseph to become houseguest with them, and so they all stayed in Bethlehem for more than a year, during which Joseph worked at odd jobs in carpentry. When Jesus was about three weeks old some priests from Ur, the Magi, came to visit and pay homage to the light of life."

"When Jesus and Mary were presented in the temple there was some fuss over the incident, and Herod came to hear of it, so he summoned the magi to give some explanation, but they managed to avoid giving him any satisfaction."

Lieu 'Murder of infant sons' "In mid October of 6 B.C. sixteen infant boys were killed in Bethlehem by Herod's order, but sympathetic persons enabled the escape of the little family, so they had left the day before, enroute to Alexandria in Egypt, where they stayed for two full years till after the death of Herod."

"On the occasion of their imminent return, a group of older friends presented Jesus with a complete copy of a Greek translation of the Hebrew scriptures, though it was not actually handed over until all efforts to persuade the little family to stay in Egypt failed to overcome their resolve to return to Palestine."

"The small family arrived in Bethlehem in September of 4 B.C., and after much discussion as to their best choice for the area in which rearing Jesus should be continued, they departed for Nazareth 4 Oct of 4 B.C., when Jesus was three. The parents agreed between no more to speak of him as a child of promise."

"On 2 April of 3 B.C. a second child was born, called James. In July of this year an outbreak of malignant intestinal disease prompted Mary to take Jesus and James to stay two months with her brother, some miles south, in Sarid."

Lieu 'Fifth Year, 2 B.C.' "In August of this year Jesus turned five, but one month before his birthday, his sister Miriam was born, on July 11. This was also the year in which Jesus started studying the writing of Aramaic, Greek, and Hebrew, using sandboxes on the roof for practice."

Lieu 'Sixth Year, 1 B.C.' "In early summer Zacharias, Elizabeth, and their son John came to visit for a few days, and the boys became friends. Jesus was admonished that prayers were properly to be of ritualistic and static form, not casual and personal, as he was wont to express his 'talking with the Father'."

Lieu 'Seventh Year, 1 A.D.' "It was an unusual year—in early January there was a two-foot fall of snow, the heaviest in a century. And in July an off-season sandstorm obscured Jesus' vision, and he fell partway down the bedroom roof stairs. More mundanely, he learned to milk the cow, and to make cheese."

Lieu 'The Eighth Year, 2 A.D.' "A dedicated student, Jesus was excused from attendance one week each month, and he used those weeks to spend time with a fisherman uncle, and on occasion, a farmer uncle. He met a teacher of math from Damascus, and spent much time on that subject for several years. He arranged also for lessons on the harp, and became proficient by the age of 11. His third brother, Simon, was born Friday evening, 14 April, 2 A.D."

Lieu 'The Ninth Year, 3 A.D.' "This year Jesus fell afoul of the Jewish law which declared all man-made images to be essentially idolatrous, and a group of elders sat in judgment of this matter. Jesus stood up to them and defended his actions, but he also volunteered to live by whatever decision Joseph might make in the matter. Joseph agreed with the elders, and Jesus so bound himself. On Thur night, 13 Sep, 3 A.D. his second sister Martha was born."

"Jesus had a good mind and expressed himself with great vigor, so gradually he became the leader of a growing group of young male friends."

Lieu 'The Tenth Year, 4 A.D.' "This year Jesus entered the advanced school in the synagogue, but it was also the first year that he started becoming aware of some intimations of his life calling, and although he asked each of his parents if they could help him in this matter, they gave him little help. In this, as in other questions Jesus put to them, they seem to have taken the wiser course—since the two of them had different views as to his destiny it would hardly help to put him in the awkward position of having to choose between them. It was another two years before he broached the subject with them again."

"The lack of direction from Mary and Joseph may have been a contributing factor in Jesus becoming the source of a lot of contentious exchanges in the synagogue—he kept Nazareth in a periodic hubbub of fuss and discussion."

"As he looked for answers Jesus developed a predilection for associating with older and more educated persons, to some discomfort of his parents—they really wondered what might be coming up next from his always searching questions."

Lieu 'Eleventh Year, 5 A.D.' "Another brother, Jude, was born 24 Jul 5 A.D. and Mary was quite ill for several weeks. This marked a turning point too, in the life of young Jesus— he would nevermore be free of mounting responsibilities; his salad days were done. He was a good size, and well built, but when some bully accosted him, Jesus would scarcely defend himself by blocking the assault, let alone deliver a punishing blow in return—he had a friend named Jacob, who was always more than ready to impose retribution. Together, they were at peace."

Lieu 'The Twelfth Year, 6 A.D.' "Throughout this year Jesus struggled with his self-knowledge, troubled by the not as yet fully apprehended fact that he had a single personality residing in a not as yet comprehended dual nature. Joseph and Mary lived and died without ever learning of his divinity."

"Jesus became aware of his two parents having different expectations as to his mission, having heard bits and pieces of their discussions on the subject, and of course he came to accept that Joseph was closer to the truth, which resulted in a rift between him and Mary that only widened as he became more self aware."

Lieu 'Thirteenth Year, 7 A.D.' "On Sunday night 9 Jan of 7 A.D. another baby brother, Amos, was born. And about the middle of February Jesus became aware that he was destined to perform a mission involving the enlightenment of man and the revelation of God. The time had come for Jesus, now graduated from the local synagogue as a son of Israel, to celebrate the Passover at Jerusalem, and be fully instituted as an Israeli citizen under the Law."

"Jesus made short work of expressing his reaction to the numerous profane activities he witnessed in the holy temple— he was shocked by the courtesans, the money changers, the sickening slaughter, and the materialistic attitude of many visitors. In turn, his parents were shocked at his many condemnations of things they had always deemed a proper part of the customary observances. There was no middle ground—Jesus tried to choke back his indignation, and his parents to hide their dismay."

Lieu 'Jesus in the Temple' "During the second day in the temple Jesus was challenged as being too young to attend the discussions with the elders, but since it had been the chazan in Nazareth who authorized his graduation as a son of Israel, the leader of the Jerusalem group accepted him here."

"Jesus asked a number of questions on the third day, such as:

1. 'Why should mothers be separated from the men in the temple?'
2. 'If God is a loving father to his children why are we slaughtering animals to gain divine favor?'
3. 'As the temple is dedicated to worship of the Father, is it consistent to harbor in it those who engage in secular trade?'
5. 'Is the expected Messiah to be a prince of the house of David, or will he be the light of life fostering a spiritual kingdom'?"

"On the fourth day Jesus was reunited with his parents, and suffered Mary's rebuke at his careless staying away on his own—and he offered his answer: 'Did you not know that I must be about my Father's business?' On their journey back towards Nazareth they paused on the brow of Olivet, where he proclaimed: 'O Jerusalem and the people thereof, what slaves you are—subservient to the Roman yoke and victim to your own traditions—but I will return to cleanse yonder temple and deliver my people from this bondage'!"

"And Mary, naturally, heard little more than the words of a militant Messiah."

Lieu 'Fourteenth Year, 8 A.D.' "Early this year Joseph launched a saving plan to pay for Jesus' long years of study in Jerusalem, expected to start in August of the following year when he would turn fifteen. All went well until Tuesday of 25 Sep. 8 A.D., when Joseph was fatally injured at work, and so Jesus became head of the household, responsible for the care and maintenance of his mother who was pregnant, and his seven siblings."

"This turn of events dealt summarily with the question of his further studies, and it was to remain true that Jesus 'sat at no man's feet.' And he was not to hear about Gabriel's visit to his mother till he learned of it from John, on the day of his baptism at John's hands, at the beginning of Jesus' public ministry."

Lieu 'Fifteenth Year, 9 A.D.' "Wednesday evening 17 April of 9 A.D. sister Ruth was born, the youngest child henceforth, and Jesus was the oldest son in a family of nine children, a heavy responsibility—by the middle of the fifteenth year (reckoned by the 20th century calendar) family savings were spent. It would soon be necessary to sell the house Joseph and a neighbor Jacob had owned."

"Being now fifteen, the age of transition from child to young man, Jesus was authorized to deliver the lesson at the Nazareth synagogue, and the audience was much impressed by his manner of doing so, and his choice of readings."

"The family's financial status continued to suffer, especially when it turned out that Herod refused any compensation for them that should have been due with the death of Joseph. They could not afford the various taxes and levies they were pressed to pay, and seizure of chattels was always a threat, so Jesus donated the Greek copy of the scriptures to the local synagogue." Here ends lesson 17.

Lieu 'Sixteenth Year, A.D. 10' "Jesus now attained the full growth that comes with adolescence, and also having to deal with the questioning and the searching that faces the transition from childhood to manhood in any culture."

Lieu 'Seventeenth Year A.D. 11'

"In this year a nationalistic movement in opposition to the taxes levied by the Romans put Jesus into two quandaries: first, the local youths were looking to him to lead them in this, and when he refused Mary viewed that decision as a betrayal of her plans for him; second, when a well-to-do Jewish money changer offered to support the family so Jesus would be free to accept the anti-Roman leadership, he still had to demur, difficult as it was."

"Jesus here lost the approbation and affection of many relatives and of the community at large, and this situation was to continue for many years."

Lieu 'Eighteenth Year, A.D. 12' "Since James was now old enough for it, Jesus took him to Jerusalem for the Passover. In September Elizabeth and John came for a visit. John was now in a position to be head of his family, his father having died some time before. The two young men discussed their respective plans and decided they would not meet again until the Father called them."

"Late in the year, 3 December, little Amos died after a week of high fever."

Lieu 'Nineteenth Year, A.D. 13' "By the beginning of this year Jesus had won his mother over to his method of disciplining the children, substituting the positive for the taboo-based customary negative—'Do thus and so, for your greater good;' not 'Do not do this and not that, for your lesser evil'."

"This year Jude was of an age to start at school, and sadly Jesus sold his harp to pay for that. No more would he enjoy the pleasure and relaxation of playing it."

"A young lady named Rebecca, now seventeen, fell in love with Jesus, but he could not make a commitment—she would become one of the women followers."

# Chapter 17

## In Whom I am well Pleased

Lieu 'The Twentieth Year, A.D. 14' "Most noteworthy this year was Jesus' prevailing on his friends at Bethany (whose mother had also been laid to rest) to celebrate their Passover without butchering a lamb for the purpose. Mary was at first quite shocked at this disregard of Moses' law, but came to accept it when Jesus assured her he would not do this in their own home."

Lieu 'Twenty-First Year, A.D. 15' "This year it was time for Joseph to attend his age of majority Passover at Jerusalem, so Jesus took him there."

Lieu 'Twenty-Second Year, A.D. 16' "This year, since carpentry was less in demand in the Nazareth area, Jesus left James in charge of the repair shop and Joseph at the home bench, while the oldest brother himself went to work for six months with a blacksmith at Sepphoris—yet another new trade, and working with gentiles was a good opportunity to learn more of how gentiles lived their lives."

"Jesus appointed James as proxy head of the family, including the finances, and henceforth Jesus made weekly payments to James."

Lieu 'Twenty-Third Year, A.D. 17' "This year it was the turn of Simon to be formally recognized as a son of Israel during the Passover at Jerusalem."

"Jesus spent much time this trip with a half-Jewish businessman from Damascus, who ended up gathering a group of like-minded scholars and bankers who joined him to collectively launch a project creating a center of religious philosophy and higher learning that would rival Alexandria, to be headed up by Jesus, who spent the last four months of this year with his friend in Damascus. But of course Jesus could not commit himself to any such moneyed enterprise."

"Mary and the rest of the family were quite at a loss to account for all these goings on, never understanding his interest in foreigners from other cultures."

Lieu 'Twenty-Fourth Year, A.D. 18' "After this year's Passover a young man from Alexandria came to Nazareth to arrange a meeting for Jesus with five very prominent Jews of Alexandria, who besought him to move to their city and set up as a religious teacher, and as assistant to the chazan in their main synagogue."

"Jesus declined their offer, saying his hour had not yet come, and also did not accept the purse they pressed upon him, saying his household was not in need, as there were strong arms and a sufficiency of will and talent to win their bread."

Lieu 'Twenty-Fifth Year, A.D. 19' "This was the year for the Jerusalem Passover ceremony and the coming of age celebration for brother Jude, and Jesus took him hence for that purpose, but Jude, hearing a Roman guard make a deprecatory remark about a Jewish girl passing by, upbraided the man in no uncertain terms, and was promptly arrested. Jesus shared his firecracker brother's two nights in prison, and pleaded his case the following morning—it would be several years before Jude was able to complete his passage into seniority as a Son of Israel."

Lieu 'Twenty-Sixth Year, A.D. 20' "This was the year of Jesus' preparation for separating from his family's upkeep, putting James in charge of all such cares from that time forward."

Lieu 'Twenty-Seventh Year, A.D. 21' "In January Jesus left home, announcing to his family that he was going to tour the cities about the Sea of Galilee. When he stopped in Capernaum, visiting with Zebedee the boatbuilder, the two of them decided to develop a new and better designed type of boat, so Jesus spent a year dedicated to this project, which was a great success."

"In October he returned briefly to Nazareth to attend Martha's wedding."

Lieu 'Twenty-Eighth Year, A.D. 22' "In March of this year Jesus took leave of his friends in Capernaum, asking John to act in his stead regarding any monies due. John did this with care and diligence."

"At Passover time this year Jesus met an Indian merchant and his adolescent son in Jerusalem, and made an agreement to travel with them for two years as teacher, adviser, and interpreter. Jesus, worried about his family in Nazareth, took payment for the first year in advance, and turned this money over to John, who later managed things so that he and his father Zebedee bought in Jesus' name a house in Capernaum, sending rent proceeds to Jesus' family in Nazareth. Jesus knew nothing about this during his long absence."

Lieu 'Twenty-Ninth Year A.D. 23' "The tour of the Roman world took much of the 28th and all of the 29th year, to 10 Dec,

A.D.23 when he said good-bye to the father Gonod, and the son Ganid, in the city of Charax. The itinerary: Caesarea, Alexandria, Lasea, Carthage, Malta, Syracuse, Messina, Naples, Capua, Rome, Tarentum, Nicopolis, Corinth, Athens, Troas, Ephesus, Rhodes, Cyprus, Antioch, Sidon, Thapsacus, Larissa, Damascus, Babylon, Ur, Susa, Charax."

"For ease of comprehension, discussions during this tour will be rendered in closer than the usual approach to the phraseology of 20th century N.America."

"It was believed by many at that time that God creates both good and evil. Jesus, in correcting this misapprehension, spoke as follows: 'There is no place in God's positive dicta for any negative evil, for evil is the immature choosing and the unthinking misstep of those who resist goodness, reject beauty, and are disloyal to truth—evil is that which is dark and untrue, and which, when embraced consciously and endorsed willfully, becomes sin'."

"Commenting on the difference between the mind of animal and human, Jesus said: 'Will is that manifestation of the human mind which enables subjective goal-seeking consciousness to express itself objectively and aspire to be Godlike."

Lieu 'Time and Space,1.' "Said Jesus: 'Time is the stream of flowing temporal events perceived by creature consciousness. Time is a name given to the succession arrangement whereby events are recognized and segregated. The universe of space is a time-related phenomenon as viewed from any interior position. On inhabited worlds Father—fragment indwelt human personality can transcend the material sequence of events, and as man progresses spiritually he develops an enlarging view of succession so that the wholeness of change is seen in greater compass and as a more unified apprehension—circular simultaneity more and more often replaces a linear sequence of consciousness'."

Lieu 'Time and Space,2.' "Said Jesus: 'Space is not merely an intellectual concept of the relatedness of material objects, for space is not empty, and mind is the only proclivity that transcends space, since space is a relatively and comparatively finite mortal conception—the nearer consciousness approaches the awareness of seven cosmic dimensions the more does the concept of space potentiality approach ultimacy. Surviving mortals achieve their ultimate settled identity in a seven-dimensional universe'."

Lieu 'The ThirtiethYear, A.D. 24' "At the end of his tour of the Roman empire Jesus stopped in Capernaum where he found James, working with John Zebedee. He forthwith turned over the house that had been bought in his name, to James."

"Having waited for Jesus' blessing, Simon and Jude held a double wedding in early March, A.D. 24, which left only Ruth, almost fifteen, at home with Mary, and it was decided that the two would move to the little house in Capernaum, and that Joseph and his family would live in and take charge of the Nazareth property."

Lieu 'Thirty-First Year, A.D. 25' "In the six weeks straddling August and September of this year Jesus prepared to confer with his Satania enemies as Joshua ben Joseph, concluding his response to their specious proposals with: 'I commit you to the adjudication of the judges of a greater universe'."

"Michael here won the unquestioned sovereignty of this local universe, which would be formally announced at his baptismal meeting with John the Baptist."

Lieu 'John, who would be Baptist' "John was a strapping lad—over six feet at the age of sixteen, and having taken the vows of a Nazarite at fourteen, he was a striking figure, with uncut flowing hair and wearing a hairy garment with leather girdle. He took the life of a shepherd, though his mother kept him informed as to the news of the day—this suddenly came to a halt when she died 17 Aug. 22 A.D. when he was twenty-eight."

"The prophet Elijah had a great influence on John—just such a stalwart and picturesque child of nature, taking a direct and blunt assault on the sins and vices of his contemporaries: he was a clear thinker and a powerful speaker."

"John settled on his mission to become the herald of the Messiah—he set out in March of A.D. 25 to launch his short but brilliant career as a public preacher."

"On Saturday evening of 12 January A.D. 26, two of Jesus' brothers, James and Jude, sought him at his work in the boatshop at Capernaum, asking him for counsel as to being baptized by John. Jesus requested that they postpone the discussion till the following day, when he would give them his answer."

"The brothers came at noon the next day, and Jesus, saying 'My hour has come—let us go to John,' laid down his tools, and the three set forth. They spent the night in the Jordan valley, joining the baptismal line Monday 14 Jan, A.D. 26."

Lieu 'John baptizes Jesus' "As John recognized Jesus he said 'But why do you come into the water to greet me?' Jesus replied 'To be subject to your baptism.' And John remonstrated 'But I have need to be baptized by you—why do you come to me?' Drawing closer, Jesus whispered to John 'Bear with me now, to set this example for my brothers, and that the people may know that my hour has come'. Thus did John baptize Jesus, on 14th January, A.D. 26, as well as the brothers James and Jude. John then dismissed the crowd, which slowly left."

"As people were leaving, the four men in the water heard a voice, saying, above Jesus: 'This is my beloved Son in whom I am well pleased'."

"The baptism by John was the final purely human act of Jesus—as John laid his hands on Jesus in this baptism the indwelling Father fragment took leave of the perfected soul of Jesus and in moments returned Personalized, chief of his kind in this local universe, seen only by Jesus, though heard by the three others."

"Jesus came out of the water in silence, departing towards the hills in the east—and none saw him for forty days."

"When Jesus did return to confer with John at the end of the forty days, he did not linger long, departing soon for Galilee, with no word of guidance for John other than to impress upon him that the Father would be his guide, as before."

"Jesus was almost halfway through his thirty-first year at this time."

"In June of this year John made bold to criticize Herod Antipas for taking the wife of another man, and so it happened that on 12<sup>th</sup> June, A.D. 26 John was put in prison. As the weeks passed, many of his followers went forth to join Jesus."

"John languished in his prison for some eighteen months with not so much as a word from Jesus—a sore test of faith, which he managed to endure."

# Chapter 18

## The Everlasting Arms

Lieu 'Forty Days of Decisions' "Jesus did not go into retirement for the purpose of fasting or for any sort of self-affliction—he was not an ascetic; rather had he come to destroy all such notions of approaching God, and to put in their place the revelation of the fatherhood of God and the brotherhood of man."

"He did not eat the first two days, but the reason was simply that he forgot to do so, being preoccupied with weightier matters, foremost of which was the final conference between his human and his divine mind, with the result that the divine mind would henceforth be his mind of action and of being, and his human mind's default response found expression as 'Not my will but yours be done'."

"Three days later, Jesus was presented with twelve legions of seraphim, and a proportionate number of every other order of universe intelligence, ready to do his bidding in any contingency. He decided not to formally embark on such a course, but instructed the Father Fragment Person to keep the heavenly host on standby in case the Father's will require that they be called on for some service."

"This was accepted, but the Fragment Person impressed on Jesus that such beings, though amenable in respect of space, could not be perfectly bound by any limitations as to time, since they have limited responsiveness thereto—in effect saying 'Your wish in all such matters will constitute the abridgment of time and the wish projected <u>is</u> existent unless the Father specifically rules otherwise'."

Erin "Tricky business, that. Good thing Jesus had two minds so he'd have some chance to keep track of the mirrors and the rabbit holes."

"The two minds, okay, but what's with those last two things?"

Erin "Oh, sorry. Lewis Carroll, you see—Alice in Wonderland, and Through the Looking Glass. Some other versions of motion sickness from shifty bearings, or, if it's more up your alley, the entanglements of a schizophrenia, where two 'minds' are apperceiving reality from unstable or even conflicting standpoints."

Lieu "Get thee behind me, Erin. We can play such games another time."


"Early Saturday morning, 23rd February, A.D. 26 Jesus came to rejoin John's company encamped at Pella. He helped an injured lad, whom he took home, and he accepted Andrew as the first of his apostles."

"Andrew's brother Simon asked Jesus to accept him as apostle, and Jesus said: 'Simon, you have great enthusiasm but I admonish you to be more careful in your speech—I would change your name to Peter'."

"James and John, sons of Zebedee, were confirmed too, as Jesus' apostles."

"The next day, on the journey to Galilee, Philip of Bethsaida and Nathaniel of Cana met the new group, and they also were summoned by Jesus, who said to Nathaniel,

'Behold a genuine Israelite, in whom there is no deceit—Follow me'."

"Jesus now was accompanied by six apostles, and they all spent the next night with Joseph in the Nazareth home, where Jesus, to the consternation of his family destroyed all that he had written, since henceforward he would only write on sand and dust."

Lieu 'The Wedding at Cana' "When all the particulars of the baptism of Jesus reached his mother she immediately saw cause therein to resurrect her fondest Messianic hopes for her eldest son, and many joined her in this vein, so that when they all went on to the wedding in Cana it seemed more of a public reception for Jesus than a wedding—the crowd was four times greater."

"As the day drew on it was small surprise that the supply of wine proved short of the amount consumed, and when the mother of the groom told Mary this the latter made bold to announce: 'Have no worry, I will speak to my son'."

"But when she went to do so he was much maligned and rebuked her firmly, so both of them spoke harsh and unkind words, till Mary burst into tears."

Erin "But we know that he turned water into wine, right?" "Yes, Erin, that is more or less what happened, but it was not any magical performance—you must remember what we said before about the abrogation of time: when Mary was so very upset that she cried, Jesus was moved to have things otherwise, and for a moment he wished that he could help her. And of course that's all that was required—in the spur of the moment he forgot to check himself, and the Father not objecting, the Son's wish resulted in water becoming wine."

Lieu "If you'd like a bit of contextual support on this question, try reading J.W.Dunne's *An Experiment with Time*, an intriguing book."

"Note now, that Jesus had almost without noticing it himself, performed one of the signs and wonders that the Messiah enthusiasts were expecting to see, so he spent another night with little sleep, pondering how he might proceed."

"Was he the promised one? Certainly he was the fulfillment of John's prediction; and equally, he was definitely the answer to the prophetic utterances of the more spiritual of the olden seers. Conscious of his divinity, he saw all this to be the Father's will—dovetailing into an harmonious and coherent sequence."

'Jesus' first consequential public appearance now was in the synagogue at Capernaum on Sabbath, 2 March, A.D. 26, and he spoke confidently about the coming of the kingdom of god. Later, in the evening he instructed his followers to go about their usual business, as he would in the boat shop, and all were to spend three hours each evening in preparation for their later duties, and this continued for four long months with the six chosen ones and his brother James."

"On Sunday 23 June of A.D. 26 Jesus enjoined the six apostles that each of them should choose a candidate to be added to their group, thus making twelve apostles, to do the work that would need doing, and in the meantime he sent: James and John to Kheresa; Andrew and Peter to

Capernaum; and Philip and Nathaniel to Tarichea—not to preach, but to do a two week tour of personal work in winning converts to the doctrine of the kingdom of god. They were all to come to the home of Zebedee for a conference at the end of their tour."

Lieu 'Twelve Apostles' "Jesus had decided, but not announced, that it would be best if none of his kin became apostles, and his brothers, of course, were disappointed, as was Mary. It was another turning point in a long list of growing disaffection between the Prince of Peace and his immediate family."

"The teaching tour of the six was quite successful, and each gave a good report of his experience, as well as announcing his choice for a new apostle."

"Andrew selected Matthew Levi, customs collector of Capernaum;

Philip chose Thomas Didymus, a fisherman of Tarichea;

James Zebedee picked Judas Alpheus, also a fisherman;

John Zebedee selected James Alpheus (twin brother to Judas), fisherman;

Peter chose Simon Zelotes, who relinquished his position with the Zealots;

Nathaniel invited Judas Iscariot, a Judean experienced in finance."

Lieu 'About Simon, Andrew's brother' "When Simon joined the apostles he was thirty years old, married, and father of three children, and lived at Bethsaida, near Capernaum, with both his mother in law and his brother Andrew forming part of the greater family cohabiting there. Both Simon and

Andrew were partners with the sons of Zebedee in the fishing business."

"Jesus had known Simon for some time when Andrew presented him to be the second apostle, so Jesus suggested the name Peter with a smile as a sort of nickname, a commonly recognized opposite to the erratic and impulsive nature of the candidate—in other words, a lightly sarcastic antonym to his known style of behavior. It would have been more a propos had Andrew been given that appellation, as he was recognized to be steady as a rock, and proved to be so."

"Peter was eloquent and dramatic. A quick thinker, he resolved issues in a flash and was ready to implement the result immediately, but at times unwisely."

Lieu 'Ordinations Twelve' "At noon of 12 January, A.D. 27, Jesus called all twelve of the apostles together, and they all went into the hills near Capernaum."

"Jesus addressed them as follows: 'My heavenly Father is not the God of Jew or gentile—many from afar will come to sit with us in his kingdom, and many of Abraham's children will refuse to enter the new brotherhood of the rule of the Father's spirit in the hearts of men.' This kingdom shall consist not in the strength of armies nor in the might of riches, but rather in the glory of the divine spirit who shall teach the minds and rule the hearts of the sons of God, in a brotherhood of love where righteousness reigns and the clarion call will be 'Peace on earth and good will to all men', "the fulfillment of the wise promises of all the prophets." And Jesus spoke further, setting forth the lessons in what we have come to know as The Sermon on the Mount."

"Note that Jesus did not direct his followers to follow a communal mode of living, nor did he formulate any economic theories—his prime purpose was to establish the kingdom of the supreme Father; enshrining the fatherhood of god and the brotherhood of men."

Lieu 'Not a Creed' "Jesus often warned his apostles against the formulation of creeds, and the establishment of enchaining traditions that would become restrictive constraints, hindering the openness of spirit he fostered."

"My children", said Jesus, "Did I come to you denouncing Moses and the prophets? No, I came not to take away what you had from your forefathers and from holy men of old, but to show you what they would have said if they had better understood the fatherhood of God and the brotherhood of men."

Lieu 'The Concept of God' "Moses taught that Yahweh is a jealous god, a god of great wrath who hates sinners and wreaks vengeance on those who break his law—Jesus, however, taught that God is a kind and compassionate father who loves all men and forgives them their sins commensurately with their faith and their readiness to live in sonship to him. The development of the concept of God from the beginning forward can be stated as follows . . .

Yahweh, the god of the Sinai clans, a jealous, petty, and a quarrelsome god

The Most High or El Elyon, as proclaimed by Melchizedek to Abraham

The Supreme Yahweh, universal creator as already seen by Isaiah

El Shaddai, god as seen by and taught among Egyptian devotees

Elohim, a plural god, as stated: In the beginning the Gods created . . . Trinity

The Father in Heaven, or the Supreme Father, the First Source and Center

Lieu 'Passover, A.D. 27 at Jerusalem' "The first day in Jerusalem Jesus went to visit with Annas, high priest friend of former years, and relative of Salome the wife of John Zebedee, but Jesus was not welcome, and departed forthwith, saying 'Fear is man's chief enslaver, and pride his great weakness; will you betray yourself into bondage to both of these?' But Annas did not reply."

"By the end of April the opposition to Jesus by Pharisees and Sadducees had become such that the Master and his apostles decided to do personal work in Bethlehem and Hebron. Jesus and Abner visited the Nazarite colony at Engedi, of which Abner had been leader when John the Baptist first started preaching. Many of this brotherhood had difficulty accepting Jesus, as he did not teach fasting and other forms of self-denial. At the end of June they returned to Jerusalem."

"A certain Simon, member of the Sanhedrin, publicly declared himself, in June of A.D. 27, as a believer in Jesus' teachings, so opposition once more welled up, and so the group spent July teaching and preaching in southern Samaria."

"Said Jesus: 'John taught you the religion of self-examination and self-denial; I come with a new message of self-forgetfulness and self control—he who rules his own self is greater than he who conquers a city'. 'Self-mastery is the measure of a man's moral nature, and by your personal faith will you become partakers of the divine nature of your supreme Father'."

Lieu 'About Prayer' "The earnest and longing repetition, when such a prayer is the sincere expression of a child of God and is uttered in faith, no matter how ill-advised or impossible of direct answer, never fails to expand the soul's capacity for spiritual receptivity. Prayer is a technique of detachment from the grind of material existence, an avenue of approach to spiritual self-realization, and individuality of intellectual and religious attainment, and is of greatest benefit when done on behalf of others, especially when they are not aware thereof."

"In October of this year there was a three week conference at the Gilboa camp between the apostles of Jesus and those of John (at Abner's urging, John had followed the example of Jesus and named twelve of the most dedicated of his followers to be his apostles.) Jesus was in attendance only in the first week."

'Resolutions of the 24 Apostles'

"1. It was decided that the 'Our Father' prayer would be taught to believers by both groups.
2. As long as John lived, both groups would meet one week every third month to review progress.
3. As the issue of the practice of baptism was not resolved jointly, two of John's apostles would henceforth travel with the apostles of Jesus to perform

baptism in the manner they had done heretofore, whereas the apostles of Jesus would teach the new believers their final instructions, the joint council having voted that the practice of baptism would be the initial outward sign of alliance with the kingdom.

4. It was decided later, that in case of John's death, his disciples would join the Jesus group, and baptism would be with water, under the accompanying injunction 'believe and be baptized'."

'Death of John the Baptist' "On the evening of 10 January, A.D. 28, by order of Herod Antipas, John was executed. On hearing this, Jesus addressed his followers, saying: 'Tonight arrange your affairs accordingly—the hour has come to proclaim the kingdom openly, with power. Tomorrow we go to Galilee'."

"Some days later, when of an evening around the home of the Zebedees in Capernaum the street was thronged with some thousand supplicants seeking the healing of their afflictions, the words 'with power' were unexpectedly realized, as Jesus once more in spirit ceding to the Father's will the outcome of this sudden quest for healing, saw as in the Cana case the almost immediate fulfillment of his scarcely formulated wish that the desire for power to the betterment of yearning mortals was enacted, and in a moment of time, 683 persons were made whole."

"From May 3 to October 3 of A.D. 28 Jesus and the apostolic party were in residence at the Zebedee home, while at the seaside not far away an encampment of some five to fifteen hundred of truth seekers, healing supplicants, and curiosity devotees, was maintained under the supervision of David Zebedee and the Alpheus twins, the sick being grouped carefully under the care of a Syrian physician named Elman. In five months several thousand attendees came and went at this self sustaining enterprise, from which none were turned away."

Lieu 'Healings and Help' "Since Jesus often visited those under Elman's care, it was almost inevitable that their improvement was ascribed to the power of Jesus, but in this setting were no such supernatural healings—there were transformations of mind and spirit as may occur in the case of faith-dominated persons who feel an allayment of fear and anxiety in empathic resonance with a kindred spirit."

"The apostle Thomas asked the Master 'Why is it necessary for men to be born of the spirit in order to enter the kingdom? Is rebirth needed to escape the control of the evil one?' Jesus replied: 'You are confused Thomas, by the doctrines of the Greeks, in that you view mankind as beginning on earth with a perfect Adam, then degenerating through sin to his present deplorable state. So how would you interpret the meaning of the record of the sons of god finding wives for themselves among the daughters of men'? But Thomas was silent."

"So Jesus said 'I have come to show that man, by entrance into the kingdom is ascending certainly and surely up to divine perfection—have you not read in the Scriptures "You are the children of the Lord your God"?"

"Similarly Nathaniel said to Jesus: 'I am at a loss to understand why the loving Father permits so much suffering to afflict his children on earth.' Jesus replied, 'You must understand that man brings down on himself many afflictions by his refusal to walk in the better ways of the divine will— they are the natural result of the life which he chooses to live. Intelligent application would enable man to overcome much of his earthly misery'. Remember, it is written: 'When you pass through the waters of affliction, I will be with you, and when you pass through the rivers of adversity, I will not forsake you'."

# Chapter 19

## Lengthening Shadows

Lieu 'The Second Tour' "On Sunday, 3 Oct AD 28 began the second public preaching tour, and it carried on until 30 Dec that year, with a schedule training the 117 new evangelists who had become part of the regular group of believers."

"David Zebedee had by this time established a central clearing station in his father's house as a headquarters for his increasingly efficient and active group of messengers who keep everyone abreast of what was happening that might be of interest to all the believers, wherever they might be or what they were doing."

"On this tour, and in times to come, it became more and more evident that instances of what might almost be called spontaneous healing were wont to take place, with no formality or any systematic recognition or cognizance of what had occurred. Every now and then Jesus might remark that he felt a touch, or a loss of power, when such things happened. Typically, if an unforeseen healing were in evidence, the Master charged the person involved to tell no one of this, but as often as not, the healed person could not comply, being too grateful to do so. We should remember that Jesus was wont to say: 'Your faith has made you whole'."

"Not all of the 117 evangelists were present at the conclusion of this tour—seventy-five were still part of the body faithful, but the others had fallen away."

Lieu 'Women Evangelists' "Just before the third preaching tour, Jesus astounded everyone by setting apart ten women for the ministering work of the kingdom—in due course two more were added, Mary Magdalene and Rebecca, the daughter of Joseph of Arimathea, bringing the total to twelve."

Erin "Like the twelve apostles!" Lieu "Exactly!"

Lieu 'The Sower Parable' "In March of the following year the evangelists tarried at Bethsaida for a time, and it was in this setting that Jesus resolved to teach in parables, choosing for the first example that of the sower, whose seeds met with such different fates depending on where they fell to ground."

"Jesus explained: 'Those who hunger for truth will have ears to hear, and will find the good news of the kingdom, but those who seek to discredit our work so that they may harm us, will find in this teaching nothing they can blame us for."

Lieu 'To Feed 5,000' "On a Wednesday afternoon of 29 March A.D. 29, Jesus and his retenue found themselves in charge of a huge crowd that had been with them on the quiet side of a large lake in the Capernaum area, and the whole assembly was in dire need of feeding. The lad Mark was told to see what he could find, and he returned with five barley loaves and two dried fishes. Jesus took the loaves, gave thanks, broke the bread and gave it to his apostles, who took and distributed it to the multitude; and likewise with the fishes. The crowd did eat and were filled, so Jesus requested the surplus should be brought back to him, and lo, there was enough to fill twelve basketfuls. They had fed five thousand guests."

"This was the first and only nature miracle which Jesus performed by way of conscious preplanning. And the crowd would proclaim him King of the Jews—but Jesus, saying 'my kingdom is not of this world,' sent them to their homes."

Lieu 'The Bread of Life' "With the approach of Passover, the band of brothers set out for more populated areas, and prepared to celebrate the feast in the new synagogue at Capernaum. Jesus was granted leave to speak and teach therein, in spite of some resistance fueled by the recent rumors of his kingship."

"At the end of the reading, Jesus, pointing to a decorative depiction of a pot of manna on a lintel, declaimed: 'You have thought that your forefathers in the wilderness ate manna— the bread of heaven—but I say to you that this was the bread of earth. While Moses did not give your fathers bread from heaven, my Father now stands ready to give you the true bread of life. And when you say to me, "Give us this living bread" I will answer: 'I am this bread of life—only yesterday did I feed you with bread for your bodies; today I offer you the bread of life for your hungry souls. Will you now take the bread of the spirit'?"

"One of the teachers from Jerusalem, a member of the Sanhedrin, rose up and asked 'Are you saying that you are the bread of heaven, and that the manna which Moses gave our fathers was not'? "And Jesus answered, 'You understood correctly, I am this bread of life, and this bread of life which I give to all who will receive is my own living and combined nature—that is my life-giving revelation to the world, and my saving gift to all nations'."

"One of the visiting Pharisees shouted at Jesus: 'How can you give us your flesh to eat or your blood to drink'? Jesus replied 'I did not teach you that my flesh is the bread of life nor that my blood is the water thereof. But I did say that my life in the flesh is a bestowal of the bread of heaven—you can become one in spirit with me even as I am one in spirit with the Father: you can be nourished by the eternal word of God, which is indeed the bread of life. The Father has sent me into the world to show how he desires to indwell and direct all men'."

"One of the Jerusalem spies spoke up, saying 'You nor your apostles wash your hands before breaking bread, and thus you break the law of the elders'."

"Said Jesus: 'you use the man made traditions to break the laws of God, as you are now doing in your speech—Amen amen I say to you 'It is not that which enters the mouth that defiles the man but rather that which leaves it'."

"Another of the Pharisees brought to Jesus a distraught youth who was possessed of a rebellious spirit, and Jesus took the lad by the hand and said: 'You know who I am; come out of him; and I charge one of your loyal fellows to see that you do not return'. Immediately the youth was normal-minded."

"It was the first case where Jesus really cast an 'evil spirit' out of a person."

Erin "So this was a midwayer taking possession of a human being?" "It does sound that way, doesn't it? But not definitely spelled out as such."

"On a Friday in early May the rulers of the Capernaum synagogue officially closed their temple to Jesus and his followers—however, their leader Jairus resigned, and openly allied himself with Jesus, a welcome positive turn amidst the abandonment by so many believers that scarcely 150 remained."

Lieu 'Synagogues Off Limits' "On May 8, A.D. 29 the Sanhedrin at Jerusalem passed a decree closing all the synagogues in Palestine to Jesus and his followers, and since this was a flagrant abuse of its authority since the synagogue for each community had been under the rule of its own board of governers, five members of the Sanhedrin forthwith resigned. The one hundred messengers dispatched to deliver this ruling made it effective in just two weeks, to all but the synagogue in Hebron, where a declaration of independence was the response—and not long after, that synagogue was destroyed by fire."

"On May 18 Herod agreed to the plan of permitting the Sanhedrin to arrest Jesus and have him tried at Jerusalem on religious charges, on condition that the Roman ruler of Judea also agreed to this proposal, and Herod signed it May 21."

'Who do men say I am?' "At noon of August 8, when Jesus and the twelve stopped for lunch, he asked them point blank, 'Who do men say that I am'?"

"They answered him with various accounts of what had been said on this subject, ranging from the tame and nondescript to various reincarnations."

"Jesus, with a sweeping gesture bunching them all together, intoned 'But who say you that I am'? At this Simon Peter, springing to his feet, exclaimed: 'You are the Deliverer, the Son of the living God'!"

"Jesus spoke: 'The hour has come when you must know the truth about me. Though I stand before you in this physical presence, I came forth from God the Father. Before Abraham was, I am. I did come forth from the Father into this world as you have known me, and I declare to you that I must presently leave this world and return to the work of my Father. And now can you understand that the Son of Man will not meet the expectations of your fathers regarding the Messiah? My kingdom is not of this world: foxes have holes and birds have nests—I do not, though he who has seen me has seen the Father, and my Father is helping me."

'Transfiguration' "On the morning of Friday, August 12 of A.D. 29, Jesus, pointing to Mount Hermon bid the twelve 'Lay in provisions for a journey to yonder mountain, where the spirit bids me go to be endowed for the finish of my work on earth. And I would take my brethren along that they may be strengthened for the trying times which will soon be upon us.'"

"Early on the morning of Monday, August 15, Jesus took Peter, James, and John with him up the slopes of Mount Hermon, where he told them of his former visits here, once after his baptism, and again in connection with Lucifer."

"Jesus had a conversation with Gabriel and the Father Melchizedek, both of them wrapped in a heavenly light, much to the amazement of the apostles, who were truly afraid, when they heard a voice say 'This is my beloved Son; give heed to him'. Jesus intimated they would see greater things than this, but their fear was not lessened by this reassurance."

"In the midst of this Jesus sought to know his Father's will, and he decided to pursue the mortal bestowal to its natural end."

Lieu 'Epilepsy; Possession' "On Tuesday morning, as Jesus and the three approached the apostolic camp, there was a crowd astir in the area—a certain James of Safed was there with his teenage son, who was doubly afflicted with epilepsy and possession by a rebellious midwayer, and they sought Jesus, hoping for healing. Simon Zelotes had made an attempt to bring about this healing, saying 'Come out of him you unclean spirit; in the name of Jesus obey me.' But this failed, the lad falling into another extreme fit."

"James of Safed implored Jesus to help the son, and Jesus replied 'Question not my Father's power of love, only the sincerity and reach of your faith. All things are possible to him who really believes'."

"James of Safed then retorted: 'Lord, I believe. I pray you, help my unbelief'."

"Taking the lad by the hand, Jesus said: 'My son, arise! Come out of him, disobedient spirit, and go not back into him'. And it was so, a double healing."

"Jesus well knew that in his absence the apostles had once again been in dispute concerning their upcoming positions in the kingdom that was to come, the kingdom headed by Jesus as triumphant Messiah—they just could not face the truth he had so often impressed upon them. And again he chastised them, adding 'Now remember what I say: the Son of Man will be put to death, but he shall rise again.' And again were they totally bewildered."

Erin "Can't help wondering if they were a bit . . . stupid?" Lieu "Not fair, Erin, not fair at all—we've been looking at all this,knowing the ending right from the beginning, so we cannot take credit for being prescient or knowledgable. Had we been in their position, who knows if we would have behaved any better."

Lieu 'The First May Be Last' "Andrew brought to Jesus a devout believer who was young and rich, named Matadormus, who would fain be one of the anointed envoys on behalf of the kingdom, but when Jesus told him he would have to give up his wealth for this to be realized, Matadormus could not bring himself to do so, and walked away downcast and sorrowful. As it turned out, he would later do exactly what Jesus suggested, and became a leader of note."

"Peter questioned what had happened with Matadormus, so Jesus told him: 'If one's wealth does not invade the precincts of the soul, it is of no consequence'."

Lieu 'The Last May Be First' "Jesus told the parable of the householder who went to the market several times to hire those who waited to be employed, and agreed with each one on a denarius for the work. When he paid the later hirelings the same amount as the earlier there was protest from the latter, but all were paid according to agreement— none were shorted; none overpaid. It was true that the later arrivals worked fewer hours than the earlier ones, but normal commerce follows a law of contract, not a law of fairness or of just desserts: the householders' being generous to the later arrivals did not give rise to a premium on the denarius that he promised the earlier ones."

Lieu 'The Seventy at Magadan' "When Jesus and the twelve returned from Jerusalem to Magadan several groups of disciples gathered there, totaling some two hundred, and in a couple of weeks reorganization and training in review led to the emergence of some seventy promising candidates for ordination."

"On the Sabbath afternoon of 19 November this group was ordained, and they were sent forth in pairs to do the work of the kingdom the very next day."

'Parting Pointers' "The seventy were admonished as follows:

1. The gospel of the kingdom must be proclaimed to all, gentile and Jew.
2. Discourage the expectation of miracles in ministering to the infirm.
3. Teach the kingdom as a brotherhood of spirit, not of pomp and power.
4. There is one commandment: love God totally, and others as yourself."

"The women's group of twelve had also trained a larger group of fifty to go out and do work in home visitations, as well as ministering to the afflicted, under the leadership of Simon Peter's wife, and they too went forth, two by two."

'Who is my Neighbor?' "A crafty lawyer asked Jesus 'What should I do to gain eternal life?' and Jesus replied 'What have you learned from Scriptures and from the best teachers?' And the leading answer was 'To love God totally, and my neighbor as myself.' The lawyer, well knowing that in Jewish law one's neighbors were defined as the children of one's people, and all others as "gentile dogs," now came to the crux of the issue, saying as he drew closer: 'But Teacher, who is my neighbor?'

Jesus then recounted the story of the man who had been robbed and beaten, had been ignored by passers-by, until one Samaritan took pity on him, bound his wounds and put him up in the nearest place of shelter, then Jesus asked 'Who proved himself neighbor to the man so afflicted?' And, hoisted by his own petard, the lawyer demurred at once, saying : 'He who helped him in his hour of need.' And so it was henceforth."

'Josiah's Healing with Intent' "Josiah had been born blind, and he begged for alms and food near the Jerusalem temple, appealing to Jesus, with Thomas and Nathaniel, without saying a word, his presence speaking for him. It was on a Sabbath, and Jesus decided to help the man so as to bring things to another crisis between him and the Sanhedrin, and it happened just so, although the day passed without serious incident, and Josiah became a teacher of the kingdom."

'The Perean Mission' "On Tuesday, 3 January, A.D. 30 Abner called the seventy new workers of the kingdom together, and charged them with the last major mission of the kingdom. It was active throughout the Perean area for a period of almost three months, and would be the final one led by Jesus, who divided his time between teaching by the camp at Pella, and assisting the king-dom workers whenever and wherever appropriate."

"This mission was different in that no miracles took place, and the kingdom workers baptized all believers right upon their accepting the gospel of Jesus."

Lieu 'About Wealth' "Said Jesus: 'Whatever else may concern the wealthy in the judgment, there will be three questions:

1. How much wealth have you?
2. How did you get your wealth? and
3. How did you use your wealth'?"

"And later: 'Devote yourself to your work and believe that both the Father and I know that you have need of your necessities. Seek but the greater thing and the lesser will be found therein; ask for the heavenly, and the earthly shall be included; the shadow is certain to follow the substance. But just beware—where your treasure is, there will your heart be also.'

'All too long have your fathers believed that prosperity was the token of divine approval, and that adversity was the proof of God's displeasure. I declare that such beliefs are superstitions. If riches evidence divine favor, why do the rich so often refuse to believe the good news from heaven'?"

'The Fate of Abner' "Of all the cities of Perea, in Philadelphia the largest group of Jews and gentiles embraced the good news of the kingdom, and the local synagogue had not been subject to the hegemony of the Jerusalem powers. In due time it became a significantly independent Christian church, under the leadership of Abner himself. After the death of Jesus the Jerusalem church, of which James the brother of Jesus became the leader, was involved in a feud with the church at Philadelphia. Eventually, after the destruction by the Romans at Jerusalem, it was Philadelphia that became the headquarters of the early church in the south and east, and similarly Antioch in the north and west."

"Abner was at variance with all the leaders of the early church. He fell out with Peter and James vis a vis the Jerusalem church; and with Paul over philosophical and theological differences. Abner was more Babylonian than Hellenic, and he resisted all attempts by Paul to remake the teachings of Jesus. In his last years Abner denounced Paul as the 'clever corruptor of the teachings of Jesus'."

"In the later years the believers at Philadelphia held more strictly to the religion of Jesus than any other group on earth." Erin 'Sounds to me as if we might look at Abner in relation to the later schism between Rome and Babylon."

Lieu "You do have your moments, dear Erin, you do have your moments."

"Abner lived to be 89, and died at Philadelphia 21 November, A.D. 74."

# Chapter 20

## Thy Kingdom Come

Lieu 'The Kingdom of God' "This is the expression we have been using to denote the teachings of Jesus regarding the full achievement of the goodness of God as relating to man, for the time being leaving to one side a sadly ambiguous epithet 'The Kingdom of Heaven,' due to the fact that the latter evokes a picture of a royal kinglike entity reigning over his subjects, who reside in a huge almost 'geographic' locale called Heaven—and which cannot quite be brought to square up with what we have learned about the 'Corps of the Finality' and their destiny."

Erin "Now hold on just a minute, first you took away the whole notion of Hell, for which you might be forgiven, but now, in an iconoclastic passion for ultra-demonic symmetry, you're casting doubt on the existence of Heaven, no less: these are the two legs the churches stand on—where are you headed, above or below your shoulders?"

Lieu "Cute, Erin, cute. Now listen; do I really have to remind you that I do little more than repeat like a phonograph the material I have received, material I was not even aware of receiving at the time? I could with good reason claim I am not responsible for what I indite, you must agree. But, I may be able to help with a selective recounting of how all this likely happened, okay?"

Erin "Do your thing my lady Lieu, show us how our Heaven was abolished."

Lieu "At Pella, on Saturday afternoon, 11 March of A.D. 30, Jesus gave a long and detailed talk on the subject of the kingdom. It seems that the Jews had settled on an interpretation of the kingdom of God/Heaven some time before the arrival of Jesus on earth, and it consisted of an eventual eternal age of God's supreme rule on earth, in which all mankind would worship Yahweh, and the Jews, as the chosen people, would intermediate between God and other men."

"This new order of things would be inaugurated after the establishment of the promised Messiah's new 'kingdom,' which would be that over the Jews per se."

"The Jews at the time of Jesus' bestowal, no matter what his ideas, his actions, and his preaching, could not relinquish some version of their essentially temporal understanding of what a kingdom had to be—endless repetition of the idea that the kingdom at issue was not and would not be of this earth, that it was and would be, a spiritual kingdom, were, to the minds of his listeners, some sort of poetic turn of phrase, a picturesque parable-to-be, for the simple minds of simple children, not to be taken too seriously by grown men or women."

"After all, how could one be an actual child of God the Father, and how could one be not only the neighbor but actually the brother of some gentile 'dog'?"

"So, Erin, how am I doing? You see the source of some misunderstanding?"

"Yes, in the few short years of Jesus' ministering, there was just not enough time to significantly change the thinking of so many tradition-bound people on so many points of difference between an earthly king and a heavenly one."

"Right, but there is another aspect to this question. You will have noticed that some of the terminology regarding astronomical matters is of a kind between the sciences as we practice them and the revelation that I have been recounting—for instance, in what I have indited, the term Paradise refers to an unimaginably huge middle portion of the central universe, which has much more to do with gravity and the control thereof than it does with the religious use of it with which we are so familiar from scripture and other revelation, where it is used as almost a synonym of Heaven, for instance when Jesus says to one of the brigands that were crucified near him that the man would be with him in Paradise—I have yet to hear of anyone thinking that the word in that dictum refers to a physical place."

Erin "No, not much argument there, not from any point of view."

"Okay. Now, it seems to me that the term Havona, which I have presented as referring to the perfect pattern universe surrounding Paradise whereon perfect beings dwell in perfect harmony, sounds much like Heaven and, although I have no proof of it, the argument might well be made that the word Havona is the source of the term 'Heaven' but who knows—it could even be the reverse."

"Yes, that did occur to me as well—seems plausible either way."

"Let us not be timid. The Christian churches, although they are certainly social arrangements of believers in the divinity of 'the Christ,' still fall far short of the ideal of the kingdom of God of which the very kernel and the inmost pith at the heart of the matter as taught by Jesus—the fatherhood of God and the loving brotherhood of man, both in a purely spiritual family sense, will prove to be the cocoon that now encapsulates what will in final bloom yield the eventual resurgence of that very fatherhood and brotherhood that it was the mission of Jesus to establish."

"His mission will not in Finality fail."

"On the forenoon of Monday, 13 March, Jesus and the apostles forsook the camp at Pella and started on a circuitous journey that would take them to Jerusalem for the Passover. And strange to relate, almost all of the thousands of believers fully expected that Jesus would declare his earthly kingdom presently."

"A warrior king would enter a city on a horse; a king proferring peace and friendship, on a donkey—Jesus entered Jerusalem on a donkey."

Lieu 'Forgiveness' "Simon Peter and James were discussing sin and the forgiveness thereof, asking the Master if it were true that the Father forgives the sin even before the sinner shows repentance, and Jesus replied: 'When a wise man understands the impulses of his fellows he will love them as brothers and will forgive them, and that is Godlike. When a child offends he will at times feel a guilty separation from his father, but the father, wiser in these things, will not be conscious of, will not feel, such a separation—sin is an experience of creature consciousness; it is not part of God's consciousness'."

Lieu 'The Final Decree' "Just before midnight on Tuesday 4 April of A.D. 30 the Sanhedrin as then constituted, officially and unanimously voted, imposing the death sentence on both Jesus and Lazarus!"

"Philip came to Jesus, saying 'Master, the feast of Passover draws near; where should we celebrate the meal?' and Jesus, summoning Peter and John, answered: 'Go to Jerusalem, follow the man with the water pitcher, and ask of him concerning the upper chamber in his house, and he will show you it is set up and ready for our use,' that being in the home of John Mark and his father."

"Judas, who had at this point already organized the betrayal of Jesus, did not know of this arrangement until he and the others arrived at the Marks' house."

"Jesus and David Zebedee knew what Judas was planning. One thing about the betrayal that is not common knowledge is the fact that Judas was acting from his personal disenchantment, not from any greedy side of his moral demise; he turned over all funds that he had in keeping as treasurer, to David Zebedee. The thirty pieces of silver were to him an insult, not a payment."

'The Last Cup' "As Jesus took the third cup of wine, the cup of blessing, he said 'Take this cup, all of you, and drink. This cup is that of my remembrance. This is the cup of the blessing of a new dispensation of grace and truth. It shall be to you the emblem of the bestowal and ministry of the divine Spirit of Truth. And I will not again drink this cup with you until I drink in new form with you in the Father's eternal kingdom'."

"Later that night, before all retired to their rest in the camp on Mt Olivet, David spoke to Jesus, saying 'Master I sent for your family, and I have word that they are tonight in Jericho, and will be here in the forenoon'. 'Let it be so, David'."

"Two contingents of armed men came to arrest Jesus, the Jewish guards of the temple; and, a concession by civil authorities, a body of Roman soldiers."

"Jesus was taken and bound, but as he was led away John Zebedee kept close to him. The Roman captain spoke: 'Roman law allows that any prisoner may have at least one friend to stand with him before the judgment bar, so this man will not be molested'. John now had something of the status of Roman counselor in the proceedings, with enough authority to kept him immune from harm."

"Since the Romans were accustomed to dealing with Annas, the former high priest of the temple, the Roman captain ordered that Jesus be taken to the palace of Annas, where in some three hours of desultory exchanges between

Jesus and Annas, no progress was made of any kind. It was during this time that Peter, in fear for his own safety, in the courtyard outside, three times denied being a follower of, or even of knowing Jesus. He did not follow when the parties went on to the palace of the current high priest, Caiaphas."

"At about three am of this Friday morning, Caiaphas summoned the Sanhedrin, and Jesus was at what might loosely be called a trial accordingly. The very meeting of the Sanhedrin at this hour and date was against the Jewish laws, and the proceedings were such as we, now in our western culture might call a kangaroo court. The charges that would be punishable by the death of Jesus were not even presented to be heard."

"When Jesus was taken to be examined by Pontius Pilate, that worthy could not think of anything very sensible either, the proceedings at this Roman palace being as sorely mismanaged as had been evident up till then. The expected rubber stamping from Pilate was not achieved."

"As fully recorded in the scriptures, this fiasco ended with the release of Barabbas and the departure of Jesus on his way to be crucified."

"Judas, after being scorned in fell derision of his claim to great rewards, was presented with a small bag of pieces of silver. In outrage he scattered them on the floor, and in an effort to hang himself from a tree on the edge of a cliff, only broke the sash he tried to use, and was smashed at the foot of the precipice."

# Chapter 21

## Thy Will Be Done

Lieu 'The Crucifixion' "Before leaving the courtyard the Roman soldiers placed the crossbeam on Jesus' shoulders—the upright timber having been transported to Golgotha ahead of time. On a white board the captain of the guard, leading the way, showed the inscription 'Jesus of Nazareth—King of the Jews'."

"The rulers of the Jews had planned to have Jesus' body thrown into the open burial pits of Gehenna, where wild beasts feasted on carrion, but Nicodemus and Joseph of Arimathea had gone to Pilate with funds, requesting the body of Jesus—Pilate refused to take the money and quickly signed the needed order."

"There was an altercation with the Jews at the foot of the cross, but the captain enforced the order from Pilate, and the body of Jesus was taken to the never yet used family tomb of Joseph, wrapped in cloths saturated with myrrh and aloes, wrapped in linen, and laid on a shelf inside the tomb."

"A Sanhedrist committee petitioned Pilate for security at the tomb, so ten Jewish guards and ten Roman soldiers were stationed there."

"John Mark brought the eleven apostles to the last supper chamber; David Zebedee stayed at the home of Nicodemus, and the women embalmers stayed at the home of Joseph of Arimathea. Mary, Ruth and Jude returned to Bethany."

Lieu 'The Resurrection of Jesus' "At two minutes past three Sunday morning 9 April of A.D. 30, the morontia form of Jesus came forth from the tomb of Joseph. At that point the physical body of Jesus was intact and undisturbed, nor was the entrance affected, as no stone had been moved. The seals of Pilate were intact and all ten guards were on duty, not having seen the morontia form emerge, it being the case that a morontia body can at times be immaterial and invisible in the style of spirit, and at other times tactile in the style of matter."

"The physical body was reduced to mere traces by the invocation of time acceleration, and midwayers rolled away the stone doorway, which frightened all of the guards to the extent that they fled pell mell to their leaders."

"It was about 3:30 in the morning when the women who planned to properly embalm Jesus arrived at the empty tomb, and Mary Magdalene went in and ascertained that the body was gone, although the wrappings still lay there. A figure they at first took to be a gardener spoke to them, and they realized it was Jesus who addressed them. They could see well enough to recognize him due to the ministry of transformers and midwayers. Jesus suggested they go to tell the apostles what was happening, which they did. Peter and John went out to see."

Lieu 'The Dispensational Resurrection' "At half past four on this Sunday morning Jesus invoked the requisite elements of the third earthly planetary dispensation roll call, the previous one having been at the time of Adam, and the first at the arrival of the planetary prince Caligastia. With the signal from

Gabriel: 'At the mandate of Michael, let the dead of this planet dispensation rise'! all the sleeping or suspension survivors since the time of Adam appeared in the halls of mansonia for morontia investiture."

"Jesus appeared to, and spoke with, key believers—of the five first appearances, Mary Magdalene witnessed four. She had become the main spokes-person for the womens' group, but proclaimed her news to all who would listen."

"About six on Friday morning of April 21, Jesus made his thirteenth appearance, and this to the apostles as they were about to beach their boat at Bethsaida, but the Master bade them toss the net to the right, and they caught over a hundred fish. It was the skill of Jesus as fisherman, not a miracle."

"This day Jesus counseled each of them person to person, as each had need, and every one had the benefit of his focused attention and advice."

"The sixteenth manifestation of Jesus took place in the courtyard of Nicodemus on Friday, 5 May at about nine in the evening. Present were: the 11 apostles, the women's corps, and about fifty leading disciples, some Greek. As he taught them he said: 'You should be stirred in your hearts by the knowledge that the dead of an age entered upon the eternal ascent soon after I arose from the tomb of Joseph'."

"Take proper note of this, Erin—to the best of our knowledge, it is the only reference made by Jesus, in all of the many addresses he gave to his followers, regarding the mass rising of the sleeping survivors at the end of an age being translated to the mansonia realms to begin the ages of learning and growing their way through the levels of morontia growth on the way to meeting the Father."

Erin "Yes, I'm sure you are right, and how startling that is, really!"

Lieu "Quite. We have no record as far as I know of Jesus teaching the apostles or disciples about the rising of innumerable 'sleeping survivors' at the end of a dispensation such as that between Adam and Michael. We must assume he did, or he could hardly expect them to understand his casual mention of it now."

'The Ascension of Jesus' "Early Thursday morning 18 May, Jesus appeared to the apostles who were about to break fast in the Mark home, and said to them: 'I am about to leave you alone in the world—the hour has come.' And he led them out to the Mount of Olives. Said he, 'Remember all I have taught you and the life I have lived among you. My love overshadows you, my spirit will dwell with you, and my peace shall abide upon you. Farewell'."

"He vanished from their sight, his disappearance no different from the others that had ended his visitations during the forty days of his morontia life on earth."

"At about noon a large number of believers gathered in the Mark home, and they suddenly became aware of a new and profound sense of spiritual joy, of security, and of confidence. And they went forth and courageously announced to all whom they encountered the new good spell, that Jesus had risen from death, had ascended into heaven, and had now sent to his apostles and disciples the Spirit of Truth, the very spirit who now inspired them with the revelation to broadcast the news of a different world and a new faith in the Messiah-Christ who would henceforth guide and lead all believers to everlasting glory in Heaven."

"And thus was born the Christian church."

# Chapter 1
## Another View

## <u>Going to Canada</u>

Goodbye then, to my invisible friend?
Whom I was just starting to know better,
Relying on, my misgivings to mend.
And challenge her waxing wit, to get her
Off her guard and so engender, foster
The missing me, to alter ego be,
Pilot run, a prototype. I've lost her!
Now all that's left is vain hyperbole.
We're poised to flee and go to see the snows
From Hispanic to Inuit, that make
The tiny Netherlands a spot that glows;
Horizon light too small to see; to take
A specious afterimage blur away
To fix, enbrain, in memory to stay.

# Chapter 2
**Another View**

## <u>A Summer Break</u>

A good year done with decent marks, so now
To ShallowsArc and summer at the mill.
An honest day for honest pay, so how
Could anyone do better, with good will.
He'd had his turns at farming work: to hay
Was hot and hard; and endless rows of corn
To hoe would make his shoulders ache all day.
Becoming just a farmer he'd forsworn.
Good to be home again, seeing girlfriend
Student nurse. Leukje's safely under wraps
So nothing untoward there should offend;
Odd noises misinterpreted, perhaps.
Would sawmilling two months give him the chance
To grow, on to the next machine advance?

# Chapter 3
## Another View

## <u>A Revelation Before</u>

Thousands of years ago the tales of old
Were gathered into revered collections,
By holy men at holy sites extolled,
Then, supplemented by semite cousins
As decades passed, they grew in verity
To last, and ever more in truth to bask.
Inspired songs so bold, as psalms they blithely
Pass into part of scripture fast, and task
The holy men into pandect to weave
This music of the soul, enshrine divine
So that posterities their thirst relieve
And to Scripture this heritage consign.
Hebrew prophets and kings made history
Which scribes embalmed right into mystery.

# Chapter 4

## Another View

## Silent upon a Peak

Silent, upon a peak in Darien,
On cliff's edge poised, a new world to behold;
Forget old rhymes, welcome shining beacon
That shows how we can parse anew, remold
The basic structure, building a new world
That never was, but had always been there,
Beneath the haze reiterating curled;
By repetition squeezed into old fare;
Familiarity breeds and seeds again;
One walks amid the fog, bearing the smog
And cannot see above or anywhen
Out of this time, out of this fen, this bog.
Kindly give us light, oh lord and bequeath
To the new child a solid rock beneath.
Thank you, Keats, for first looking . . .

# Chapter 5
## Another View

## <u>The Inward Path</u>

Supreme adventure of them all; we raise
Objective pinnacle so tall and proud.
We cannot wait; with bated breath, apace
We haste to leave the port, our ends avowed.
But soon the mansion worlds will give us pause
Redacting shortcomings galore; before
We can go on we must complete the mortal clause,
Round out the space-time ken of life ashore.
With that achieved henceforth we face the goal
To perfect be, we work and learn and strive
From sphere to world anew, to self control
The mule head Adam in us all, contrive
To reach the goal and foster spirit whole,
Until one day we meet Him, soul to Soul.

# Chapter 6
**Another View**

## The Trinity

A common maxim tried and true is that
Two heads are better than one, obvious
Then that the two would yield to three right flat,
Even though only a common purpose
Group-holds the three together in a loose
Confederation by targeted goal.
Another case: the three may one produce,
Create a being, singleminded, whole;
With power absolute and one in scope,
And all creation must perforce await
Portent Trinity judgment in the hope
That order new, by fiat fell create,
Commemorate, the greatest good by far
That ever could be wished, upon a star.

# Chapter 7
**Another View**

## <u>The Power</u>

Modernity coming twenty miles out
By way of electric wire to come;
Down some trees, cut smaller wood, brush burnout.
The way is clear so bring it here, freedom
From coal oil lamps and flashlight trips at night
From cold and dark outhouse, uneasy stops;
Instead we'll have a privacy in light
Just flip the flush and out she flops and drops
Down to the brand new septic tank below
The house, with any smell contained by drain
Enclosed in soil, and leaves our sweet chateau
A little bastion, isolate domain.
The shed beside the drive would now have power
And Erin use his tools at any hour.

# Chapter 8
## Another View

## <u>Trinitized Sons of God</u>

Mighty Messengers all have made their way
Unto the Corps of the Finality;
Just ordinary people who display
Though tempted thick and thin a constancy
To persevere and keep the flame alight,
Sustain the fainting hope in spite of all
Setbacks galore that pull them into fright
And shake them to the core to drop the ball
But no, there's work to do, they cannot fail,
So perseverance saves the day and wins
For them triumphant victory, all hail!
In benediction have they beat their sins.
By that same path in High Authority
Came other men to fame, convincingly.

# Chapter 9
## Another View

## <u>Power by the Hour</u>

Universe charged with the grandeur of God,
Flaming forth like glittering from shook foil . . .
No: picayune, just too petty, slipshod;
Miltonian song would better uncoil,
Stentorian cadence to rise above
Mentoring the mortal imaging small,
In timid tones cooing just like a dove,
Fears to embrace; the colossus enthrall.
Inspiration fails to match the matter;
Still piteous selves  just bound up too tight
To cast off restraints, become the author,
To break from his bonds, engage the floodlight,
That heaven above welcome in its grace
The news that mankind outshines his mean race.
Thank you G.M. Hopkins

# Chapter 10
## Another View

## <u>Many Mansions</u>

'In my father's house are many mansions'
Said Jesus; a puzzle to modern ears.
To most of us a house is home, curtains
Privately closing out the world for years
While cloistered separation peace awaits.
So how could mansions be inside a home
When mansions evoke castles and estates?
Twixt poetry and prose disjoint we roam,
Or seek between two languages to weld
A common thought, despite the strange nuance
In that old text's confusion still upheld;
In every new edition, same response.
'Let there be light' has had to wait as well
Till revelations eons later tell.

# Chapter 11
## Another View

## <u>The Lucifer Rebellion</u>

What insanity is this—a brilliant
Leader of the heav'nly hosts to rebel
Against the Godhead foundant Trinity,
The glorious source of all the good, repel.
By silly subterfuge no less, ill will
Could actually blind his reason, make blank
That intellect renowned, that mind instill
With notions of such vanity, embank
Beyond all bounds the spark of decency
That must have glowed in hidden piteous glimpse
Below, beneath a hubris so blithely
Piled on high that even mortal eye crimps
In disbelief profound, for chaos bound
As all is lost in sophistries unsound.

# Chapter 12

## Another View

## The Dawn of Willful Man

The grand plan is no sooner launched, and life
Crawls up the muddy seaside shore to try
The newfound raspy air, is joined in strife
With others climbing there, and may not lie
At ease. The ages come and go, transform
Fourfooted beasts that seek to rise, to free
Two thinking hands. Two mammal glands will warm
The primate apechild form, so man will be.
All this, then, god created, god directed
And god sustained, all good and all foreseen,
How could it just go wrong; how, unprotected,
From godly failure fall, and man, so keen
To learn from planet prince, is given dross,
Abandoned in a fog, and at a loss.

# Chapter 13
## Another View

## From Planet Prince to very Devil

Lucifer stumbled when he denied that
The Father was the source of personhood,
And, less conceivable, had not begat
The great whole-all, since pre-time He ne'er could
As Father have existed. A no thing
In a nowhere cannot a self create
Much less another be, with just basing
All that on airy nothing. An estate
Without foundation cannot just have form,
Or any substance with right of passage.
Some words in Satan's ear suffice to warm
A henchman's will to publish this portent,
Pervert the cause of heaven itself, and blight
The hope of many a world in blackest night.

# Chapter 14

## Another View

## Andonite to SonGod to Midway

Two corporeals pair, but really mate not
With bodies from savages material
An offspring get, invisible but fraught
With quintal motile power to baffle
A sighted ordinary man voiceless.
Spirit powers mind, and mind runs matter;
Matter man to midwayer is bootless.
Yet spirit bright can be misled and augur
A mass defect to Caligastia snake,
Thus most midwayers broke away, a shame.
And caused Material Sons the worst heartbreak
Abet Adamic default and quit claim
From universal mission to uplift,
To build anew such bodies, God's good gift.

# Chapter 15
## Another View

## <u>The Path of Moses</u>

A lady of the pharaoh's kin took vows,
Wedding a worthy Semite man at arms
And in due course their hybrid son avows
To set his people free, and thus alarms
The whole administration. 'Let us go!'
He cries and soon the lines are drawn, apart
In warlike pose, as talking heads aglow
With righteousness practice their art to thwart
Th' outrageous fools in opposition formed.
Then all withdraw and in small conference
The principals present their case, prewarned
That remonstrance will not trump a silence.
And silent, mighty Moses leads the flight
Of kinsmen, henchmen, kith and kin, at night.

# Chapter 16
## Another View

## Jesus, 16 to 21

When Jesus was but fifteen years of age
His father Joseph, hurt at work, had died,
And Herod would not pay th'outstanding wage,
Saying nothing was due—the old fox lied.
So there was Jesus, eldest child of nine,
Creator of this universe, now faced
With being brother and father, in fine
Quandary, destitute of means, debased
In abject poverty. By sweat of brow
He must provide, those hungry mouths placate,
And erstwhile be to Mary SON somehow;
Son of Man and Prince of Peace to enstate.
Oh Jesus Lord we pray for thee, that thou,
Though still a child thyself, will win somehow.

# Chapter 17
## Another View

## <u>In Whom I am well Pleased</u>

Rough-hewn nazarite John baptizes Jesus
In the Jordan water, to mark the break
Unto god-man's divinity blameless.
Henceforth that human mind will not partake
In any critique point, but ablate
The crux in default to the Father's will.
The Father spark now fuses with helpmate,
To personality-cum soul fulfill.
God's good will be done—Jesus' hour has come
Now can he teach the fatherhood of God
And brotherhood of man in pure freedom,
With no more trades and sacrificial blood.
So hail to thee blithe spirit and be free
In peace and blessed happiness to be.
Thank you, P.B. Shelley

# Chapter 18
**Another View**

## <u>The Everlasting Arms</u>

The toddler learns his dad is full of might,
So, full of faith expects his fall's arrest
In failsafe instant grasp t'alight alright,
And moments later gently be caressed.
But human father sometimes fails to catch
The little one, whose faith is then impaired
As paradigms of mighty dad mismatch
Reality's sterner mien, sometime prepared
To let a fall appall the tender child.
Assurances cannot quite fix the fault
And growing mind be not so soon beguiled;
We learn to not the mortal man exalt.
No human being can forever live
And yield what everlasting arms will give."

# Chapter 19
## Another View

## <u>Lengthening Shadows</u>

With one eye on his final days to come
Jesus tried to prepare his followers,
To build a solid core of the seldom
Flustered ones, the tried and faithful sowers
Of promise, with clear and forward resolve
To join with listener's yearning want, quiet
Uncertainty at root and thus involve
The inmost wanting deepest heart, audit
What all along had achingly been there
To be assured of better things to come,
Be part and portion of the holy heir
And build a centrum, wholly blessed become.
The leader to them, Abner resolute
In faith and mind, would cavillers refute.

# Chapter 20
**Another View**

## Thy Kingdom Come

Hell has been replaced by fairy nothing;
The Devil's kingdom is now snuffing out.
A kingdom needs a king to make it sing;
Kingdom of Heaven now is up for doubt.
Finaliters in outer space will strive
To make whole brand new universes gyre
And homopitheci to bring alive.
But heav'n cannot in mundane mud bemire
Halcyon days, ambrosial fare, and golden harps;
Cannot bedome the slimy slush with blue,
Or beatific song make just from sharps.
The heav'n of Christian hope does not come true
We must align our sight with all our might;
So spirit power imbues God's kingdom bright.

# Chapter 21
## Another View

## <u>Thy Will Be Done</u>

The Michael Son who bowed to none now hangs
Upon the cross, and earth is singled out
Amongst ten million to suffer the pangs
Of everlasting shame, the Lord sold out
For hardnecked reputation, and the rule
Of custom labels us: World of the Cross.
That good men blind do nothing brave is cruel
Right past the grasp, gives thugs the double-cross.
The kindest and the greatest soul we met
Or ever could imagine, lord above;
The God Son Father of us all, we let
The evil-minded set on purest dove.
Oh Lord of all be with us yet and let
Us better be for what we can't forget.

Readers interested in learning more about the material
presented by Lieu, please google the word 'urantia.'